THE CATHOLIC UNIVERSITY OF AMERICA
CANON LAW STUDIES
Number 52

THE APPOINTMENT OF PASTORS

A DISSERTATION

Submitted to the Faculty of Canon Law of the Catholic University of America in Partial Fulfillment of the Requirements for the Degree of Doctor of Both Laws

BY

JOHN JOSEPH COADY, S. T. D., J. U. L., A. M.
Priest of the Archdiocese of Baltimore

THE CATHOLIC UNIVERSITY OF AMERICA
WASHINGTON, D. C.
1929

Nihil Obstat:

PHILLIPUS BERNARDINI,

Censor Deputatus.

Washingtonii, D. C., die 15 Maii, 1929.

Imprimatur:

✠ MICHAEL J. CURLEY,

Archiepiscopus Baltimorensis.

Baltimorae, die 15 Maii, 1929.

WASHINGTON TYPOGRAPHERS, INC.
WASHINGTON, D. C.

TABLE OF CONTENTS

CHAPTER EIGHTEEN

THE APPOINTMENT OF PASTORS

Introduction

In the vast field of church organization and ecclesiastical law the subject of pastors is a most important one. They represent a sort of third degree of the hierarchy of jurisdiction [1] in ecclesiastical law. Properly speaking, they cannot be counted in the hierarchy at all, but are included in it only in an imperfect sense, for their jurisdiction extends not to the external but altogether to the internal forum. The pastor has a recognized position in the Church, for though the pastorate is of ecclesiastical institution, nevertheless the Bishop cannot abolish it. The office of the pastor and of the priest is very ancient indeed. The priesthood was instituted by Christ Himself at the Last Supper, *"Hoc facite in meam commemorationem."* [2] The Council of Trent defined: *"Si quis dixerit in Ecclesia catholica non esse hierarchiam divina ordinatione institutam, quae constat ex episcopis, presbyteris et ministris, A. S.* [3] From Scripture it is deduced that there were priests as well as bishops from the very beginning of Christianity. St. Paul ordained presbyters who had the right to ordain other presbyters. Those presbyters who were only priests and not bishops, were chosen from the elders and were charged with the duty of prayer and the administration of the Sacraments.[4] The hierarchical organization which placed a bishop over priests, deacons and faithful is clearly defined from the second century onward.[5] Deacons assisted in the regulating of temporal affairs, in maintaining good order in the assemblies and in ecclesiastical

---

[1] See Wernz-Vidal II, p. 763. Praenotiones.

[2] Luc. XXII, 19.

[3] Conc. Trid. sess. XIII, Can. 6.

[4] S. Jacobi Epist. V, 12-16; Ad Titum, I, 5: Act. Apost. XIV, 1, 3, 6, 20, 22; XX, 17, 28; Apoc. II, 1; III, 22; I Ad Timotheum, V, 19; Cf. Lesetre, La Paroisse, pp. 4-5.

[5] Cf. Tanquerey, Synopsis Theol. Dogmat., Pars Secunda, p. 562, 563; S. Epiphanius Contra Heres., LXXV, 4; M. P. G. XLII, 507; M. P. G., I, 803.

discipline. The priests who were their superiors, cooperate in the offering of Mass and are charged especially with instructing the Faithful. St. Jerome writing later asks: What is there that a bishop can do and a priest cannot do except to ordain?[6] In those early days of the Catholic Church the priest's function was defined as it is today, and he carried on his ministry, which was as necessary then as it is now.

The position of a pastor in the Church today is naturally a most necessary one, as it is he who directly ministers to the spiritual needs of the flock of Christ. He comes in the closest and most constant contact with the sheep of that flock. At the present time the Church's law concerning the pastor is clearer and more precise than ever before in its history. Much, indeed, has been written on this subject, both from the historical and from the juridical point of view, because the topic is vast, and much more extensive and complicated than one would at first imagine, and the historical sources are both numerous and lengthy. It is proposed here to treat but one point of the topic of pastors, and in the present essay to sketch somewhat briefly the historical development that has led up to the present exact legislation on the manner of appointing to this office. There will be found, of course, in it that evolution which marks the progress of any healthy growth. Difficulties and dangers are removed, the system is perfected, until at this date the ruling is definite and detailed, conformable to analogous conditions in all modern forms of government, and what is best of all, a satisfactory avoidance of any kind of partiality.

To attempt to treat the question of the original methods of appointing one to this office without, at the same time, touching on the origin of parishes, were to attempt the impossible. So closely are the two related that they cannot be studied but somewhat jointly at their inception, for only then can at all be realized the reasons for the changes and development in the Church's attitude to the one and the other. One can never interpret the text without the context, nor appreciate any historical question without its proper orientation.

Unless then, there should be too long an introduction to a subject that in itself is vitally interesting to readers who are, in all probability, impatient to delve into this matter itself, a

[6] S. Hieronymi Comment. in Tit., I, 4, M. P. L., XXVI, 561.

word of explanation for the plan to be followed in this treatise will replace a longer preface. Instead of taking separately the various requirements of the appointment and showing the gradual development of each by itself, it is preferable to treat the subject *"in globo"* and afterwards to summarize briefly what refers to each. Otherwise, repetition would be necessary and the treatise would be much too long, for these various phases interlap in such a way that with each it would be necessary to recall a great deal that had been said of the others.

Schulte in his *"Geschichte der Quellen und Literatur des kanons,"* says that fifty-seven authors have already written on the subject of pastors. Since his day a great many more have been added to that number. The author realizes that he has undertaken that upon which many have written from various angles before him. He does not pretend to have produced a work that is in every respect original. Nor does he claim to have treated exhaustively the subject that has been his object of study during the past two years. His attendance at lectures and his duties as Curate in one of the largest parishes in the Nation's Capital, together with his initiation into the absorbing deeper studies of Canon Law would have made that impossible. But under the wise guidance of the Faculty of Canon Law at the Catholic University of America, he has been able to produce what is contained in these pages. He wishes, therefore, to take this occasion to express his deep gratitude to Monsignor Bernardini, Doctor Valentine Schaaf, O. F. M., and Doctor Louis Motry, for their kind assistance and criticism in the preparation of this dissertation.

CHAPTER I

Etymology and History of Words, "Parochus, Parochia, Paroecia"

First of all a word must be said about the etymological derivation of the expressions parish and pastor, or more properly, of the Latin terms used in the Church's law, *"parochus"* and *"parochia"* (*"paroecia"*) which are variously translated into the many languages of our day. What shall be found is that their present signification is of rather late origin. What then was the term used of old to express this present signification, and what was the earliest signification of the present terms?

It is disputed whether the nomenclature *"parochus"* and *"paroecia"* are Latin words derived from the Greek *παροικία*, *παροικέω*, or *παρέχω*. *Παροικέω* to live near, and consequently *παροικία* signifies a dwelling or a territory. Stolz in his learned disquisitions on *"Paroecia und Parochus,"* [1] after an exhaustive research in Greek philology, gives a very plausible argument for taking the meaning of *πάροικοι* in the sense of sojourners in a strange land. He gives as a proof many Biblical citations where the word *παροικέω* is to be taken in this sense. Truly, this is the clear meaning of the passages of the New Treatment and of the Old to which he refers, but why could not the word be taken otherwise in its more literal Greek signification of neighbor, or those who dwell nearby? Those who live near a particular church where the *Πάροικοι* and the pastor was the *πάροχος* or *"parochus."* The word *"parochus"* is really an abbreviation used at the time of its application in our sense, from "(*Sacerdos*) *parochitanus*," which was written "parochus." The accent replaces the elided letters. Does it not seem much more likely that the term is derived from the Greek word *παροικέω* than the word *παρέχω*, which means praebeo, i. e., to serve, to offer? To derive it from *παρέχω* seems rather too much of an *"a posteriori"*

[1] Theologische Quartalschrift Tuebingen, LXXXIX (1907); XCV (1913) p. 193; CVII (1926) pp. 1-8.

point of view, or an *argumentum convenientiae.* The reasoning for this point of view is by analogy; for among the nations of ancient times the one who offered hospitality to the representatives of other peoples, i. e., legates, etc., was called *"parochus,"* that is, a sort of innkeeper.[2] Thus the pastor did the same thing in a spiritual sense for the Christians.

Be that as it may, whatever be the true derivation of the technical expressions in ecclesiastical law, *"parochus," "paroecia," "parochia,"* [3] were not interpreted as we now understand them until very much later, centuries even, after the parish was recognized as an authentic ecclesiastical institution. There are two meanings for the word "paroecia" (parochia) in its earliest Christian use. First, it denoted that territory under the administration of the bishop.[4] Bouix, in his excellent work, *"De Parocho,"* gives several short quotations which support this meaning: "Episcopo non licet *alienam parochiam,* propria relicta pervadere."[5] "Constituit (S. Xixtus) ut quicumque episcopus evocatus fuerit ad sedem Romanam apostolicam, rediens *ad parochiam* non susciperetur nisi cum formatis," i. e., testimonial letters.[6] "Unusquisque episcopus *parochiam suam* perscrutari nitatur." [7] Even as late as 1215, in the IV Lateran Council, the same application is made of the word in the third canon; in place of "propria dioecesi," the word "propria *parochia* (paroecia) is found." "Licet," writes Marius Lupus,[8] "antiquissimum sit *"parochiae"* (*paroeciae*) nomen ad ecclesias de quibus agimus indicandas, *parochi* e contrario vocabulum *hac*

---

[2] See Barbosa, "De Officiis et Postestate Parochi," Rome 1774, pars. 1, Cap. 1, §1.

[3] According to Smith the mediaeval spelling "parochia," which is a constant variant for "paroecia" and seems to have arisen from a derivation from the classical "parochus," which has been revised in modern times by Baur, Liber Der Ursprung des Episcopats, p. 78, but is altogether untenable; cf. Dictionary of Christian Antiquities, word, "parish."

[4] A distinction sometimes appears between the "paroecia" of a simple bishop, and the diocese or "provincia" of a Metropolitan, e. g. S. Bonifac. Mogunt. Epist. 49, ad Zachariam, A. D. 742, Migne, P. L. vol. 89, 714. cf. Smith, word "parish."

[5] Can. Apost. 14 (13); cf. Hefele, A History of the Councils of the Church, I, p. 463.

[6] Lib. Pontif. in vita Xisti about A. D. 117, cf. Bouix, De Parocho, Ed. 1880, p. 8.

[7] Conc. Turon. about A. D. 813, can. 13, cf. Bouix, De Parocho, p. 10.

[8] Marii Lupi Bergomatis Ecclesiae Dissertatio, I a. cap. 8; cf. Bouix "De Parocho." Ed. 1880, p. 6.

in significatione recens prorsus est, et primo proximis solummodo superioribus saeculis usurpatum." The second meaning of the word is that in use today, i. e., the pastor of a parish. According to Stolz in the articles already referred to, this use is found first only in the years 1490 to 1493, and occurs in Spain with reference to parish records.[9] Even the Council of Trent, surprising to say, in some places where one might expect to find the word *"parochus"* uses an equivalent, yet, it was this same council which gave sanction to the present meaning of the word, and consequently the position that the technical expression now holds in ecclesiastical terminology.[10] According to De Luca the word *"parish"* began to be used first in the fourth century, and by the sixth century is commonly used for a rural congregation, *"Coeptum est saeculo circiter quarto, sed nonnisi saeculo sexto ejusmodi ruralibus a pagis ecclesiis nomen paroeciae factum est commune."* [11]

When the office of pastor is spoken of previously to this time, it is referred to in the scope of such language as: *"dioecesani presbyteri, parochiarum presbyter, parochiales sacerdotes, presbyteri plebium* or *plebani, presbyteri villani* or *forenses* or *parochitani, presbyteri baptismalium ecclesiarum, curati, sacerdotes proprii, rectores,"* and they are even at times called *"pastores."* [12] However, all these are descriptive circumlocutions that yield finally to the technical term *"parochus,"* after the fifteenth century.

---

[9] Op. cit., CVII, 1926, pp. 1-8.

[10] Counc. of Trent, Sess. XXIV, *De Ref.*, cap. 18.

[11] De Beneficiis, N. 306.

[12] Cf. De Meester, Juris Canonici et Juris Civilis Compendium, II, 242, footnote 1; Rossi, De Paroecia, p. 3, n. 3.

CHAPTER II

Parishes Not Found in First Three Centuries

If the purpose of the first part of this essay, which is to trace the history and development of the appointment of pastors, is rightly to be fulfilled, then it is advisable to go back to the origin of parishes. Naturally, the first appointment was made when the first parish was started. Of course, the historical beginnings of parishes and parish priests are difficult to ascertain. No one can point to this place or that time in history and say, "Here for the first time a priest and not a bishop was the local pastor," or "There for the first time, the small unit, parish-and-priest idea came into actual being." There is question in all this of jurisdiction and ecclesiastical institution,[1] and not of orders and divine institution, and the field of inquiry into beginnings is largely speculative. A writer of the 18th century, Bohemerus,[2] says: "Those who have written *ex professo* on the origin of parishes furnish plenty of matter for refutation, but if the truth must be told they rather obscure than throw any light on the origin in question." He goes on further to say that though the origin cannot be determined, the source idea was contemporary with the beginning of special temple building for the celebration of the Christian Mysteries.

In this matter, however, one cannot exclude a consideration of the New Testament, the books of which have not only a doctrinal, but also an historical value. In the Acts of the Apostles, and in the Epistles of St. Paul, and in the Apocalypse frequent mention of churches in cities and in states, and of bishops and of priests is found. Priests and churches in country districts are never spoken of. St. Paul, writing to Titus, whom he had left at Crete, says: That he had done so purposely "ut

[1] For a refutation of the view that parishes are of divine origin; cf. Bouix, De Parocho, Pars. 1, pp. 42-164. De Meester, Op. Cit., p. 245. Art. II, Chelodi, Jus de Personis, p. 369; Rossi, De Paroecia, p. 61 seqq.

[2] Bohemerus, Jus Parochiale; quoted by Murray, The Present Juridical Status of Parishes in the United States, p. 4.

constituat *per civitates* presbyteros."[3] But, he does not establish them, nor command them to be established outside of cities. Perhaps, this is why only in the towns the presbyters are found, and practically only one in each town, and all were to be consecrated bishops. They were called presbyters and bishops[4] promiscuously and indiscriminately, so that nothing can be concluded from the use of the word *"presbyter"* as to the origin of parish priests. It is clear that at this time there were enough bishops or presbyters for each city to have one of its own, but certainly the smaller towns and villages did not. Though the first laborers in the vineyard of the Lord were few in number, their zeal was unbounded, and through their apostolic ministry and preaching, The Word of God was soon spread, and the kingdom of God increased.

In chronological order the next source of information is the writings of the earliest fathers. Quotations to the point might be multiplied, but for the sake of brevity, let it suffice to mention only two—St. Ignatius of Antioch and St. Justin Martyr. From them it appears that still there was no such thing as parish or parish priest, at least as it is understood today. Church organization at that time was rather rudimentary. During the first three centuries the bishop alone was the pastor, and the whole diocese was his parish, and the cathedral was his parish church.[5] St. Ignatius addresses his letters to the churches of large cities. These he strives to keep united to himself, and he never speaks in them of priests in country places, nor does he regard churches as being in charge of any but bishops. St. Justin is even clearer, and tells us that those who live near the city always come to the city churches on Sundays to take part in the divine worship, which is carried on by the bishop. Deacons were sent to carry the Blessed Sacrament to those unable to come to church.[6] Traces of the same facts are to be met with in St. Cyprian.[7] Nor

---

[3] Titus, V, 5.

[4] Thomassinus: Vetus et Nova Ecclesiae Disciplina; De Parochis: Pars. I, Lib. II, Cap. XXI, n. 1; Smith: Dict. of Christ. Antiquities, Art. Parish.

[5] (St. Ignatius) Epist. ad Philadelphienses N. 4. Apud Rouet de Journel, E. Patristicum, pp. 13-23; Eodem loco, pp. 99, 212.

[6] Apud Rouet de Journel, Enchridion, p. 50, St. Justinus, Apol. I, 67; cf. Apol. II. l. c.

[7] Eodem loco, pp. 199-212.

do the canons of the Apostles speak in a different strain.[8] They say that bishops, priests and deacons are to be found together at the cathedral church. Together, in fact, they compose what was later known as the *"presbyterium"* or *"concilium,"* i. e., the senate of the bishop, and assisted him in the rule and administration of the diocese. Contemporaneous church history discloses the fact that priests and deacons were sent frequently to evangelize and minister to the spiritual wants of the faithful. But, this was only a transitory office and they were entirely at the disposal of the bishop. Not yet then can one say that the origin of the parish in the modern sense of the word [9] has been reached.

In this matter a quotation form Ferraris ought to be considered—*"Parochiae antiquitus non erant distinctae: sed episcopus curam animarum totius dioecesis, per sacerdotes pro suo libitu missos et ad nutum amobiles administrabat."* [10] Bargilliat in his Praelectiones Juris Cannonici, n. 835, repeats practically the same thing: "Primis ecclesiae saeculis, nulli exstitere parochi qui certa et stabili sede *proprium populum ac territorium* haberent sed in civitate dumtaxat episcopali *una* erat ecclesia, ad quam fideles sive in urbe, sive in agris degentes die dominica conveniebant; erat totius dioecesis *pastor* et episcopus, qui in animarium salute procuranda, ubi opus esset, presbyterorum opera utebatur; et propterea tota dioecesis merito dicebatur *parochia,* ut con stat, e. g., can 14 Apost."

---

[8] Can. Apost. Can. 15, Can. 32. Cf. Hefele, A Hist. of the Councils of the Church, I, pp. 464, 471.

[9] Cf. Koudelka, Pastors, Their Rights and Duties, 7; Thomassinus Vetus et Nova Disciplina Ecclesiae I, lib. II; Nardi, Dei Parrochi, I, cap. 12, II, cap. 22, 25, 32; Devoti, Institut. Canon. tom. I, lib. I, tit. 3, Sec. 10; Bouix De Parocho, pp. 1-175; Ferraris, Bibliotheca, "Parochia" n. 7; Soglia, Institut. Jur. Priv. I, cap. I, Sec. 25; Aichner, Comp. Jur. Eccles. (6 ed.), 422; Wernz, Jus. Decret. II; Sec. 821; Billot, De Ecclesia Christi, III, 150; Duschene, Christian Worship, Chap. I; Bargilliat, Praelect. Jur. Canon. II, Sec. 835; Imbart de la Tour, Les Paroisses Rurales, cap. 1-3; Battifol, La Paix Constant. et le Cath. Cap. 2; Revue des Questions Historiques, LXXVIII, 643; Vacant-Mangenot, Dict. de Theologie Cath. col. 2430; Maroto, Institut. Jur. Canon. II, 97; Raia, De Parochis, 4; Ayrhinac, Constitution of the Church, 294; Fanfani, De Jure Paroch., 7; Monitore Ecclesiae. (1925), 304; Rossi, De Paroecia, 7-14.

[10] Prompta Bibliotheca, word, "parochia" n. 7.

CHAPTER III

Parishes Found in Fourth Century for First Time

When it pleased the good God to snatch his Spouse, the church from the most cruel persecutions by which for so long a time the faith of the Christians had been so valiantly tried, and through Constantine the Great to place it on a mountain as a light to guide the nations, the number of the faithful became so great that one bishop could not preach the Gospel and administer the Sacraments to this great concourse of people in one city, and so small an edifice as one church could not hold them. Thus the Church was forced to provide means to meet the needs of the times. So from the fourth century other churches arose besides the episcopal cathedrals, with priests who administered to the people. For on account of the constantly increasing number of particular communities of converts, or the great difficulty of getting to the episcopal church, and many other causes, the bishops judged it opportune to open independent or auxiliary churches and to them sent priests, *"chorepiscopi,"* [1] or deacons, to exercise the ministerial powers within certain limits. The chorepiscopi of course were of a rank superior to either priest or deacon.

It might be said that in the respect of territorial divisions the church simply followed the example of the civil government.[2] There was a suburban and rural organization of the Roman empire. In the more civilized countries of that empire each important city had a district called a *"regio,"* surrounding it within which its magistrates might exercise jurisdiction.[3] Such districts often included nearby villages and hamlets which thus formed dependencies of the city. Moreover, there were also independent communities in rural districts which had their own officers and sometimes their own territory. Now, as has been

[1] Cf. Funk, Manual of Church History, I, 179, n. 62.
[2] This is the opinion of Smith, cf. Dict. of Christ. Antiq.
[3] Dig. 50, 16, 239. Ed. Mommsen-Kreuger, 1922.

said, by the end of the third century the religion of Christ had penetrated to the majority of these suburban and rural communities, and provision had to be made for them in the general organization of the Church. As may be suspected this provision varied considerably at different times and in different countries. In Syria, for example, it was sometimes the practice to attach a small town for ecclesiastical purposes to a neighboring large town.[4] In this way, Bethlehem was attached to Jerusalem. But more commonly in Syria, and some parts of Asia Minor, it appears to have become the practice, as early as the fourth century to appoint presbyters and deacons for small towns and country districts, who were in some respects on a lower footing than the presbyters and deacons of the[5] city churches and who were superintendent by the *"chorepiscopi"* (rural or country bishops).[6] These latter in turn were in some respects subordinate to the city bishops.

"Chorepiscopi," or country bishops exercising jurisdiction over the smaller towns or villages seem not to have existed in northern Africa. Clearly, both from the fact that the bishops there were so numerous, and from the taunts that were thrown out on both sides in the Donatists' controversy, it can be concluded with certainty that bishops of full rank were ordinarily appointed there wherever a Christian community existed.[7] Even in our own day the titles of many of those extinct African Sees have been retained for titular bishops who have no dioceses of their own. At the same time there are traces of the system that afterwards came more generally to prevail, as St. Augustine in Epistle 209 speaks of a "Castellum" which formed an outlying dependency of the bishop of Hippo: "Antea ibi nunquam episcopus fuit, sed simul cum contigua sibi regione ad paroeciam Hipponensis ecclesiae pertinebat." In the district around Alexandria the villages were entrusted to presbyters under the superintendence of the bishop of Alexandria. Athanasius mentions

---

[4] Sulp. Sever, Dial. 1, 8 ed. Halm, p. 159, cf. Smith "Parish."

[5] Conc. Neo-Caes. C. 13 Circa 314, Hefele, I. 229, Antioch, C. 8, Hefele, II, 6.

[6] Conc. Ancyra C. 13; Neo-Caes. C. 13, Antioch C. 10; Basil Epist. 54 (181). Hefele—History of Councils, II, pp. 211, 229; II 6.

[7] Cf. Cath. Encyclopedia, Art. Donatists, vol. V.

ten such villages, and also tells us that a bishop visited them.[8]

The circumstances under which Christianity spread in Gaul and Spain and the elaborate civil organization with which it found itself in contact in these countries led to the growth and consolidation of the parochial system which has since become permanent in the western church. Most likely in these countries the true religion did not penetrate into the country districts and the rural communes until long after its complete organization in the chief towns. These towns consequently became missionary centers. Presbyters and deacons were sent into the "*castella*" and "*vici*" partly to preach and partly to minister to the scattered Christians who were to be found there. That they did not go far from the towns and that they did not give to Christians the full advantages of Christian worship is evidenced by their having to return to the city churches every Saturday in order to assist at the services on Sunday.[9] By degrees the Christian of these country districts became more numerous, but by that time the tendency to limit the number of bishops became felt. The office of bishop had become more important. Its dignity would only be impaired by creating a bishop as in primitive times for every new community. Presbyters and deacons could easily be detached from the staff of the city churches, and deputed to serve the country churches, but always "*ad libitum episcopi.*" Their mission now was not merely "*ad praedicandum,*" but also "*ad regendum,*" i. e., to exercise ecclesiastical discipline. At first they were on the roll of the city church and supported by the bishop. They could be recalled by him and reattached to the city church. So late as the Council of Emerida A. D. 666, this was the fact. Gradually they became fixed in the several districts or paroeciae. As such they were called "cardinal" (*cardinales*), a term which was also applied to the permanent chaplains of endowed oratories[10] and was ultimately succeeded in the case of almost all churches by the term diocesan.[11] Could this be the reason why today the expres-

---

[8] St. Athanas., Apol. C. Arian., C. 63, vol. I, p. 143; c. 85, vol. I, p. 158; M. P. G., XXV, 247-410.

[9] Conc. Tarrac. A. D. 516, C-7, Cf. Hefele, A History of the Councils of the Church, IV, p. 103.

[10] Greg. M. Epist. XII, n. 11, M. P. L. LXXV.

[11] Cf. Hefele—History of the Councils, I, II, III, IV; Conc. Agath. can. 22; Conc. Tarac can. 13. Also the term *parachitani, paroeciani,*

sion "incardinated," is used of the priests who belong to a certain diocese?[12]

---

parochiales, Conc. Emerit. can. 18, 3d Conc. Tolet. can. 4; 7th Tolet. c. 4; 9th Tolet. c. 20; also *locales* 3d Tolet. c. 2; also *forastieri* Conc. Marti Brac. c. 15. Cf. Smith, word "parish."

[12] The Latin etymology of the word gives the Latin equivalent of hinge, hence priests who were attached to a district were hinged to it. So a priest in a diocese to which he has been "incardinated." The "cardinals" of the Church today all are attached to a titular church in Rome. That *cardinalis* in this use, which was transferred from certain civil offices under the empire, means fixed is rightly maintained by Gothofred, ad Cod. Theodos 12, 6, 7; Bocking, Notitia Dign. Orient. C. 5, 2, vol. I, pp. 24, 205, it is shown, e. g., by a letter of Pope Zachary to Pippin (Epist. 8, C. 15, Migne, P. L., vol. LXXXIX, 935) who will not allow a *"presbyter cardinalis"* to be appointed on a private estate, but rules that whenever masses are required in private oratories a presbyter must be specially asked for from the bishop. The other Latin meaning of *"cardinalis"* (i.e., praecipuus, according to Serv. ad Virg. Aen. I-135) is less applicable to either its civil or its eccleciastical use.

CHAPTER IV

The First Parishes Are Rural Parishes

Such is the outline of the obscure genesis of the parochial system. "When it came finally to prevail, it tended to absorb into itself the other systems upon which Christian communities had been organized, and only after struggles which extended far into the middle ages and not without the cooperation of civil powers was the net work of its elaborate organization spread over the whole of the western Christian world." [1] Despite the fact that it is so very difficult to point out the exact period that parishes started, Thomassinus thinks that they started in the middle of the fourth century, and Marius Lupus is inclined to believe that it was somewhat sooner. It seems safe to state that certain signs of parishes and parish organization did not appear before the fourth century.[2] Let it be noted, too, that this statement regards only parishes of the rural or suburban districts and the villages which were included in such districts.

In reality one can say that parish organizations began in country places certainly about the fourth century, though Barbosa seems to hold without very good proof that they arose earlier. According to him, Pope St. Dionysius (A. D. 259-268) is the first to make territorial divisions: "Antiquitus *parochiae* distinctae non erant set episcopi omnes dicebantur totius dioecesis animarum curam habere, et omnes illius decimas percipiebant et inter se et alios clericos dependebant, quia reliqui clerici de manu episcopi percipiebant et curam exercebant . . . Sed postea cum augeretur populus Christianus Dionysius Papa XXIV post B. Petrum, singulas ecclesias singulis Sac-

[1] Cf. Smith, Dictionary of Christian Antiquities, word "Parish."

[2] Thomassinus, Vetus et Nova Ecclesiae Disciplina, P. I. Lib. II, Cap. 22, N. 3; Bouix, De Parocho, Pars. I, C-6, p. 44; on page 22, C. IV, Bouix says Marius Lupus holds for the earlier origin. Wernz, Jus Decretalium, Vol. 2, p. 689; Vecchiotti, Institutiones Canonicae, Vol. I, p. 328.

erdotibus assignavit ut unusquisque *proprium* haberet territorium, nec unus alterius fines ingrederetur."[3]

It is none the less true then, that the rural parish came first, since when the word "*paroecia* (*parochia*)" ceased to be synonymous with diocese it is defined as the rural territory under the care of a presbyter, but never as city territory: "Quamquam usus inolevit, ut *parochiae* nunc aliae sint urbanae, aliae rusticae, aliter olim res se habuit; nam rusticarum proprium id nomen erat, ideoque *parochias* civitatibus opponebant."[4] Dionysius Petavius writes in the same strain: "hujusmodi ergo *paroeciarum* institutum, vel ut vulgo loquuntur, *parochiarum,* dixi in animadversiones ad Epiphanium, prius in agris et extra urbes, quam in urbibus usurpatum videri."[5]

The East possessed a resident clergy sooner than the West. City parishes, of course, were formed only much later than those in the country districts, with the exception of the cities of Rome and Alexandria; in the episcopal cities they did not appear before a thousand years.[6] The bishop's church was during all the while the only parish church, and all had to come thither to fulfil their parochial duties. Even in those places where churches were started in the fourth century their multiplication was not rapid. From the fifth to the eighth century many chapels were built, but these could not be called parish churches since they were dependent upon the principal church of the village or hamlet. After the eight century they spread more rapidly, and in the eleventh century they arose in the episcopal cities. The first steps in this direction were taken in Gaul and then in Italy.[7]

The remark has already been made that as regards the cities Rome and Alexandria, they formed exceptions to the general fact of early parish development. St. Optatus, at the end of

---

[3] Barbosa, De Officio et Potestate Parochi, Par. 1, cap. 1, n. 17-18. Could this not refer to the defining of limits for dioceses?

[4] Sirmondus, De Asimo, cap. 5, tom. 4, cf. Marius Lupus Dissert. II, in Bouix, p. 28.

[5] Dionysius Petavius, Theologica Dogmata, De Ecc. Hierarchia, lib. 2, c. XII, vol. 7, p. 633.

[6] Bouix-De Parocho., par. I—Caput V et seqq.—All modern authors are of this same opinion. Wernz-Vidal, Jus Cannonicum, II, p. 768; Chelodi, Jus De Personis, p. 369; Rossi, De Paroecia, p. 11, Seqq.; Vermeersch-Creusen, Epitome, I, p. 309.

[7] Cf. Murray, Status of Parishes in United States, c. II.

the fourth century, refers to the forty basilicas of the city of Rome,[8] and according to St. Epiphanius about the same time in the city of Alexandria each quarter had its own church and its own presbyters.[9] The secondary churches were often attended by members of the bishop's "presbyterium," and even when they had priests or deacons attached to them, they remained subordinate to the mother church, for the bishop reserved to himself the administration of the sacraments and the celebration of liturgical functions. Except, perhaps, in a few places like these, urban parishes did not become independent with full parochial rights until about the ninth century.[10]

---

[8] De Schism, Donat. II, 4. Migne, PL., XI, 883-1082.

[9] Adv. Haereses, 68, 1, cf. M.P.G., XLII, 507; cf. Sozomen, H. E., I, 15.

[10] Mourret, Histoire de l 'Eglise, vol. 3, p. 336. Revue des Questions Historiques (1905), p. 645.

CHAPTER V

Manner of Appointment to First Parishes; Influenced by Founder of Churches

When one begins to speak of the appointments to any of these places later than the time when the priests were sent thither on temporary missions, one must take into consideration the regulations for ordination in early times. In the twenty-first canon of the synod of Arles in Gaul at the beginning of the fourth century, there is found a decision that a deacon or a priest must not leave the church of his ordination and these together with all inferior ministers cannot go from one church to another: *"ut ubi quisque ordinatur, ibi permaneat."* [1] The same proposition appears in the Apostolic Canons 13-14 and 15, and also in the Council of Nice, Canon 15. Munchen says explicitly that this refers not to the diocese, but to the church.

One must remember that in those early days a bishop or priest gathered around him usually those who intended to serve in the vineyard of the Lord, sometimes at a very youthful age. These he trained himself,[2] in theological knowledge and church discipline until finally when they had attained the proper age, which was about thirty [3] years, and achieved the proper degree of knowledge, such candidates for the priesthood, or orders, had to be examined by the bishop. Sometimes, too, a bishop entrusted the education of aspirants to orders to others, but superintended it himself.[4] If, on being examined by the bishop, they

---

[1] Cf. Hefele: A History of Christian Councils from Original Documents; I, 185. Under Synod of Arles. Dr. Munchen founds his opinion on the twenty-seventh canon of the Synod of Elvira. Cf. eodem loco, p. 185, footnote 2. From this also does it follow, that one might be for a life time stationed in the same parish, since appointment came with ordination.

[2] Cf. Imbart de la Tour, P. 64. Pope Celestine insisted on this: *that parish priests should come from the parish.* The Council of Vaison A. D. 529-C. 1, ordered priests to gather aspirants and train them. Cf. Hefele IV, 169-170.

[3] Synod of Neo-Caesares (314-325) Can. 71; Cf. Hefele I, p. 228.

[4] Cf. Imbart de la Tour, p. 64.

were found satisfactory, they were by him admitted to Sacred Orders, and remained in the church for which they had been ordained. The candidate was conducted usually by an archdeacon to the bishop who examined him on his life, on his morals, and on his knowledge.[5] The priest should know the Creed, the Canons, the Penitential Book, as well as liturgy, and should be able to read and comment upon the Gospels and the homilies of the Fathers.

Already, in the very earliest ages of church government there was some conflict between the congregation and the hierarchy as regards the choice of certain ecclesiastics as parish priests. According to the Corpus Juris, XIX, Causa VII, Q-1, and in the synod of Laodicea (341-381), Canon 13,[6] the choice of those to be appointed to the priesthood, and consequently to the Church, shall not rest with the multitude entirely. Evidently, the people had some share in the appointment and *Van Espen*[7] affirms this. The eighth general council refused the right of popular election to the Greek Church. The change from popular election did not take place in the Western Church probably until the eleventh century.[8] On the other hand it seems from

[5] Boretius, pp. 109-234, in Imbart de la Tour, p. 138.

[6] Cf. Hefele—Vol. II—p. 308.

[7] Van Espen: Commentarius in Canones, Vol. II, pp. 161 seqq.

[8] This change in the Western Church at this time is probably due to the development of benefices. "The history of benefices is of somewhat greater importance because of its influence on the development of the pastoral office. . . . Benefices or the right given permanently by the Church to a cleric to receive revenues from ecclesiastical goods because of the performance of some spiritual service, were the result of a gradual development which began in the sixth century, as is now the common opinion. By the ninth century it had become the practice of the Church to attach permanently a certain amount of temporal possessions to the pastoral office itself, and not to the person as had hitherto been the custom, the revenues of which were to furnish the encumbent a means of livelihood. In the eleventh century, however, the custom of community life among the clergy began to disappear, and this brought about a division of the ecclesiastical goods so that a certain amount was attached to each office, thus giving a great impetus to the development of the system of benefices." Pugliese, The Administrative Remov. of Pastors; cf. Schmalzgrueber, Jus Eccles. Univers. III, 5, II; Schmidt, Thes. Jur. Eccles. sive Diss. III, 224; Pyrrhus Corradus, Prax. Benef. I, cap. I, Garcia, De Benefic. Eccles. I, cap. I, n. 10; Santi, Praelect. Jur. Canon. III, De Praecariis. 15; Thomass. Vet. et Nov. Discip. Eccles. III, 2, cap. 12-35; Devoti, Institut. Canon. 1, 2. 14; Sanguinetti, Jur. Eccles. Priv. Institut. II, 10; Soglia, Institut. Jur. Priv. II, Sec. 81. Vecchiotti, Institut. Canon. II, 3, Sec. 66; Aichner, Compend. Jur. Eccles. (6 ed.) 254; Wernz. Jus.

the synod of Antioch in 341 that the appointment of the priests is certainly in the hands of the bishop.[9] Sometimes the "chorepiscopus" could appoint, but as said before, he in turn received his appointment from the bishop. Besides his nominations were confined to the inferior clergy up to the rank of subdeacon.[10]

Once a priest had been appointed by the bishop he must stay in the place of such appointment, and far from changing to another charge without his permission, he cannot even travel without a special permission.[11] The Council of Chalcedon in 451 says that a cleric enrolled in two churches at the same time, i. e., "in that for which he was ordained, and that to which as the greater he had removed from motives of ambition, must be sent back to the church for which he was ordained." [12]

Coordinate with the normal formation of Christian communities by aggregation of the Christians of the city or the district was the custom of erecting places of worship upon the estates of landed proprietors. Devotion to martyrs had prompted the faithful to erect chapels on their tombs. In the first instance, there appears to have been no restrictions upon the erection of such places of worship. The civil law for fiscal reasons required the officers of such churches to be taken from the estate,[13] but otherwise until the middle of the sixth century left their appointments entirely free. It is not clear whether the Council of Chalcedon, Canon 4, which forbids the erection of monastic oratories [14] without the consent of the bishop of a city refers to these churches; if as appears most probable from the general tenor of the canon, it does not refer to them, the earlier restrictions upon their erection will be found in Justinian, Novella 67 about the year 540. This Novella requires both the consent

---

Decret. II, Sec. 245; Claeys-Bouaert, De Can. Cleri Saec. Obed. 286. Imbart de la Tour, Les Paroisses Rurales, 65; Pastor, Tract. de Benef. et Can. Eccles. I, I; Ayrninac, Constitution of the Church, 296 & 311; "Benefice," Greagh, John T., Catholic Encyclopedia, II, Canon. Contemp. XXXIV, 22; Acta Sanctae Sedis, III, 509.

[9] Synod of Antioch *"In Encaeniis,"* Cans. 3, 5, 7, 8. Cf. Hefele, II, 68-69.

[10] Eodem loco C. 10.

[11] Eodem loco C. 7.

[12] Cf. Hefele III, pp. 396-7, Counc. of Chalcedon C. 10. Gratian, C. 2, CXXI, Qu. 1; and C. 2, C. 21, Qu. 2, Sess. 15.

[13] Law of Arcadius & Honorius A. D. 398, Cod. Theodos. 16, 2, 23; Cod. Just. 1, 3, 11.

[14] See Hefele, III, pp. 389, 390.

of the bishop as a safeguard against the multiplication of heretical churches, and a sufficient endowment. In the West there are few traces of them until the sixth century; but from that time on they become more numerous. In some cases there were private chapels erected for the convenience of the owners of the estates, and this regulation was made, that although divine service might for the sake of convenience (*propter fatigationem familiae*) be performed in them on ordinary days, yet on the greater festivals resort must be had to the church of the parish or the city.[15] In other cases they appear to have had districts assigned to them, and so to have become country parishes. Hence the Fourth Council of Orleans,[16] A. D. 541, c. 26, speaks of "*Parochiae* in potentum domibus," and c. 33, "Si quis in agro suo aut habet aut postulet habere dioecesim . . .", and the Ninth Council of Toledo, A. D. 655, c. 2, deals with the case of "ecclesiae parochiales" which had been founded by private persons.

The two points which were insisted upon as regards the two classes of privately founded churches were: That they should be under the control of the bishop, and that they should be sufficiently endowed.[17] But the freedom with which in early times churches were founded in country districts, without interfering with the right of any other church came to be restricted when the greater part of the christianized West came to be covered with a network not only of diocesan but also of parochial organization. After a country district had been constituted into a parish, and especially after the payment of the tithes and fees by the people of such a district to the church of that parish had become a matter not of voluntary offering but of legal obligation, the foundation of a new church within the limits or on the borders of such a parish tended to be regarded with disfavor. Pope Zachary writing to Pipin about the year 741 will not allow churches on private estates to have, even when

---

[15] Conc. Agath. A. D. 506; c. 21; I Arvern. A. D. 535, c. 14. Cf. Hefele, IV, pp. 80, 192. Cf. Mansi, VIII, p. 865.

[16] Hefele, A History of the Councils of the Church, Vol. III, p. 213.

[17] The former of these rules appears first in the Council of Orleans, A. D. 511, C. 17; Hefele IV, p. 213, the latter was enacted by the Council of Orleans, A. D. 541, c. 33, Hefele IV, p. 214. A good example of the kind of endowment required is afforded by St. Greg. M. Epist. 12, II. For Council of Toledo 655, Cf. Hefele IV, p. 471.

endowed, baptistries or cardinal presbyters. The bishop is to consecrate them without the usual solemn mass and to send a priest to perform services as occasions require. The Carolingian Capitularies [18] allow the erection of churches by private persons with the consent of the bishop, but they are careful to provide that the former dues to the original church shall not be interfered with.[19]

The jurisdiction, therefore, of bishops over parishes and over privately founded churches, which be they within or without the limits of parishes, were within the district over which a bishop's authority was assumed to extend, was not established without many struggles. In early times another factor that must be taken into consideration, to understand the Church's legislation, is that presbyters had claimed the right to detach themselves from the churches of which they were presbyters and to set up altars where they pleased. Ultimately a presbyter who set up an altar without the consent of his bishop was *ipso facto* excommunicated, and if this separation from the rest of the Christian communities failed to deter him, resort was had, probably, for the first time in ecclesiastical history, to the secular arm.[20]

---

[18] Karoli M. Capit. ad Salz, A. D. 803, C. 3; Pertz, Capitularia, vol. I, p. 124; Mon. Ger. Hist. et Leges.

[19] Zach. Epist. 7, ad Pipin, c. 15; Migne P. L. LXXXIX, 935.

[20] Conc. Antioch, A. D. 341, can. 5; can. Apost. c. 31: See Hefele, vol. II, p. 177; I, p. 471.

CHAPTER VI

Traces of Popular Election

The theory which from the first seems to have governed all interpretations of the mind of the original church to the subsequently formed communities in the same cities, and to suburban or rural communities, was that officers of these communities were still part of the one original organization. The presbyterium of the bishop was formed, not only of those presbyters who assisted him in the ordinary administration of his own church, but of all presbyters who were in the same jurisdiction.[1] In course of time, no doubt, a distinction between these two classes of presbyters was made, and in the later middle ages the presbyters of the cathedral came to assume, not only the functions which had originally belonged to the presbyters of the diocese, but also in some cases those of the bishop himself. Under the bishop came the archpresbyter, or dean of the cathedral, and the dean of the country districts, who was called the archdeacon.

The rural clergy were in a state of rigorous dependence. It was from the bishop that each pastor held his powers and his title. In receiving them the titular must take an oath of obedience. The canons had besides reserved to the chief of the diocese certain attributes in the government of the church. He must, first of all, watch over his priests and inform himself of the purity of their faith, their morals, and their preaching. The pastor depended, moreover, on the archdeacon, or the rural dean. The whole government reposed on one idea, to insure obedience. This system of government aided the success of the Church's propagation and permanence, because of its admirably detailed organization, based on perfect discipline and cooperation.[2]

This legislation had also created guarantees. It recognized

[1] Cf. Imbart de la Tour, Cap. 1-3.

[2] Cf. Imbart de la Tour, Cap. 1-5.

certain rights for all. The first force of the rural clergy was to be chosen partly by others besides his own chief. The great principle *"of election"* was recognized by the Church and applied in the appointment of parishes. It had its consequences in the form of patronage. Every founder of a church had a right to choose the titular of that church. Also a number of monasteries and chapters and lords could present a candidate for the parishes which they had endowed. In the free parishes this right was exercised by the inhabitants. The faithful who had constructed and endowed the church presented to the bishop the rector whom they themselves had chosen.[3] In his chapters addressed to the archdeacon of the diocese of Rheims, Hincmar writes: "If I am away institute provisionally the dean who has been chosen till the choice comes to my knowledge, and is confirmed or changed by my decision."[4] The bishop then, as this text very well indicates, did not nominate. He confined himself to conferring orders and powers on the candidate of the community, provided he was satisfactory, or approved of the election of one already ordained. Care must be taken not to imagine that this popular choice was according to any of our modern systems. The *"electio"* of the parish priest must have very much resembled that of the encumbent of the episcopal dignity. There is no need to look for a voting nor a majority count. There is a text which is said to belong to a patron church, and from which it can be surmised that when a vacancy arose in a parish the inhabitants were to inform the archdeacon of it, and ask his permission to call a meeting.[5] The election took place, doubtlessly, in an assembly composed of villagers and of the parish clergy, under the presidency of the archdeacon or dean. Choosing ought to have offered little difficulty, for it has already been mentioned that each parish of any importance had its own college of clerics, that is, priests, deacons, etc. Now the

---

[3] Marca Hispanica, p. 825, cf. Imbart de la Tour, Les Paroisses, etc. Marca Hispanica is a History of Catalonia, Spain, written by Pierre Marca in 17th Cent. Cf. Cath. Encyc., vol. IX, 637 B.

[4] Migne, Tom. CXXV, p. 803, *"Si ego in longinquo sum, decanum illum qui electus est interim constituite, donec ad meam notitiam electio illa referatur et mea constitutione aut confirmetur aut immuteteur."*

[5] Zeumer, Formulae, p. 261, "Inditium ad archdiaconum" found in the Formulae Solicae Merkelianae, also Zeumer, p. 170. In Mon. Ger. Hist.; et Leges; Cf. Imbart de la Tour, p. 137.

usage obtained of selecting from amongst this rural clergy the one who was to govern the parish.

The election might fall on a priest, and in this case, he was installed by the archdeacon.[6] Often, even a simple cleric could be chosen. The one elected had then to be taken to the bishop to receive from his hands ordination to the priesthood, and ecclesiastical investiture. The ceremony was a public one, and the delegates of the vacant parish could be convoked for the occasion. After the examination which has already been referred to, the bishop addressed himself to the people, and asked for their testimony and their assent. The people replied, "He is worthy." The cleric was now ordained following the liturgical formulas, and the Mass ended. He received the libellus of his ordination, and the title which was given him.

One could also obtain a parish by prescription. If a priest in good faith had been acting as a pastor of a certain parish for thirty years, then it became his by right. *"Ut qui. . . . parochiam per triginta annos sine alicujus interpolatione tenuerit, jura perpetua possideat."* [7]

However valuable and sincere should be the popular consensus in an election the church did not disarm the hierarchy against a bad choice. She had sought to exclude the incapable and unworthy. Further no cleric could enter the priesthood before the age of thirty, and deaconship before twenty-five.[8] Bishops were forbidden to ordain illiterates, but as to the indigent, they were not excluded from the priesthood, but once promoted to the priesthood or deaconship, they could not acquire church property in their own name.[9] The hierarchy showed itself unfavorable to the ordination of serfs, much to the displeasure of the lords, for these entrusted willingly to their serfs the direction of their churches, and at the same time they wished to keep these ordained priests still their serfs. Such a fact one can

[6] For the publicity of ordinations cf. Hincmar "Adversus Hincmarum Lungunensem Libellus," Migne P. L., Tom. CXXVI, p. 563.

[7] Cf. Imbart de la Tour, p. 127 seqq. On p. 136, N. 2 Capit, a Sacerdotibus proposita, c. 17.

[8] Synodus Franconofortensis A. D. 794, c. 49; Capit. Missionum A. D. 802, c. 26, Caput Ecclesiasticum A. D. 818, c. 6, cf. Imbart de la Tour, p. 138, Mon. Ger. Hist., Ed. A. Boretius.

[9] Admonitio generalis, A. D. 789, c. 21-2; Hinsmar, Literae data Hedenulfo, Migne P. L., Tom. CXXVI, p. 273, cf. Imbart de la Tour, Les Paroisses, etc., p. 140.

easily imagine would be detrimental to their positions as priests. The only solution to such a difficulty was that the serfs thus ordained should be given their freedom. Civil law refused to consider the ordination of serfs especially if they received Orders in bad faith.[10] Besides these cases, the bishops were never bound to confer an office on an ecclesiastic who was considered unfit for it.[11]

---

[10] Cf. Imbart de la Tour, Les Paroisses Rurales, p. 311, who quotes a capitular of 818 Formulae Imperiales, Zeumer.

[11] According to "Novella" 57, cap. 2; Nov. 123, cap. 18. If unworthy clerics had been chosen, the bishop of the place, could and was obliged freely to appoint those whom he considered more fit.

CHAPTER VII

How Feudalism Affected Appointments

A priest was for life attached to the church for which he had been ordained. This union nothing could break without the form prescribed by the canons. The patron of a church could choose the titular, but he could not remove him from his charge, and even the bishop was advised to consider seriously the case of a priest whom he wished to depose.[1] It would seem then that a priest once ordained by a bishop, should always receive his appointment from that bishop.

The Church in its councils and in its laws had traced the ideal of the priest. She wished him to be free. So had forbidden him to enter the servitude of the lords and she had forbidden the lords, likewise, to attack his liberty. She wished, moreover, that the priest be well instructed and pure. Many efforts had been made to give to the clergy of the country, learning as a necessary virtue. She demanded of him the knowledge of church canons, of the Scriptures, and of chant. She had created for his use conferences, confided to his care the public schools and had called upon him for devotion to the work of alleviating human miseries. But despite the efforts of the Church abuses soon insinuated themselves. Priests sought by many ways to escape this permanency in office. Aspirations less noble than the ideal of the Church snuffed out in some the desire to conquer souls. Many of the rural priests aspired to a too great independence, some quit their parishes and roved through the diocese, without wishing to be attached to any title. Others through ambition or pressed by poverty in order to advance themselves to a better position in life subjected themselves to the lords. They sought recommendations to obtain from them a benefice and deserted their own charge for the chapel of the chateau. Thus, the

[1] Cf. Imbart de la Tour, Cap. I-5. Quotes a capitulary of 803, n. 13, Boretius, p. 107. Migne P. L., CXXVI, p. 231 and CXXV, p. 1108. Capitulary of Aix (809) c. 21.

clergy, too, submitted themselves to the system of feudalism. This fact, that the clergy used such means to seek easier posts, changed somewhat the relationship which had been established between the bishop and his clergy. Private churches were not withdrawn from the authority of the bishop, but yet they seemed at times to have had other masters, though only the bishop should have been master; so that the question of the mode in which the presbyter, or other chief officer of a parish was appointed in early times, is one upon which only scanty evidence exists, for we can find no clear historical reason why such a state of affairs should have come about. It is probable upon general grounds, that such appointments did not form an exception to the general rule, which at first required an election by the people and an approval by the bishop, and which afterwards allowed the clergy or the bishop to nominate, and the people merely to approve. But the endowment of parishes by private individuals, and the interweaving of the parochial with the canonical and monastic systems, so far overlaid the primitive practice that there was in the later middle ages only a small proportion of parishes in which the people had any real share in either the election or approval of the parish priest.[2]

[2] Cf. Smith—Hist. of Christian Antiquities, word, "parish." It seems that such an undercurrent as the concession accorded the private individual who endowed a parish, defeated the purpose of the somewhat vague legislation. Else why would there be so *many pretexts* for priests who obtain the parish or church wanted, rather than the one to which they had been destined by ordination?

CHAPTER VIII

Recognition of the Right of Patronage

When one speaks of the cases of priests who outwitted their ecclesiastical superiors by obtaining other charges through the favor of founders of particular churches, one approaches the origin of patronage which gradually appears in the Church as an offshoot of the privilege or consideration shown a benefactor. By the ninth century are found texts referring to it. Then it became something definite, though it was not really defined until the twelfth century. After that it did not change much. Traces of it are still found in some countries, but in France where it had been so strong, it was abolished in 1791. About its origin there is no exact information. Some think that the Germans brought it into France. This is the opinion of Stutz in his ingenious Dissertation, "*Die Eigenkirche als Element des Mittelalterlich-germanischen Kirchenrechtes*" (Berlin, 1895). But it must be remembered that patronage was not an institution peculiar to the Germans, and that in France, too, were found basilicas and oratories on private estates under patronage.

No document is cited in proof of this, and many contradict it. Some, on the other hand, think it to be an ecclesiastical institution, but this was not created by legislative measure in the beginning any more than was the parish itself. There is no council that established it. The first canon laws which speak of it, find it already established. On the contrary it seems that the patronage of churches takes its beginning from a number of usages, that had already sprung up. One fact of its origin is known, the foundation of a sanctuary on a domain. Sometimes too it was a chapel built at the place of burial of a martyr. This was done by the lord of the domain or by some devout Christian. From this fact came little by little the juridical rules, which formed patronage such as the Church recognized it. This fact is very ancient. It is not special to Christianity. It was a pagan custom that each proprietor raised on his domains, sanctuaries, sacella, dedicated to the local or domestic divinities. From the fourth century, Christian possessors built on their estates, "oratoria." There was in the code of Theodosius some texts that refer to these edifices, but Catholics were not the only ones to build them: "Ecclesiae quae in possessionibus, ut assolet, diversorum . . . sunt constitutae."[1] The first legislation concerning this matter is somewhat indirect.[2] It refers to a bishop who builds such a chapel in another bishop's diocese. It says that the bishop founder will please to have the cleric he chooses ordained by the bishop of the place, or if he is already ordained, he will obtain the permission of that ordinary for his functions. And all the government of the church will be under the bishop in whose diocese the church has been erected. Laymen who build such churches are forbidden to call in a bishop other than the one of the place for the ordination. The Council of Arles in 451 repeats the same legislation. This is the origin of patronage. The founder of the church could not take it nor the clergy attached to it away from the bishop of the place. By patronage the church desired it to be understood that the founder has the privilege of presenting a candidate for the place, but this took no rights away from the bishop of the place. It means, simply, that the choice of the cleric is to be made from the clergy of the parish, but the founder could make the choice which was to be ratified by the bishop. In one instance the inhabitants, and in the other, the founder presented to the bishop the priest desired for the charge.[3] Just when and how did patronage start our data is vague, and rather negative than positive.

It seems that in Spain in the sixth century the right of presentation had not been recognized at all. The first mention of this right is made in the ninth Council of Toledo, 655. In France, the Council of Orleans, in 511, recalls that all the basilicas constructed in different places remained under the diocesan bishop. In the fifth century, the Church is less concerned about defining the rights of the founders than of keeping the churches under the strict rule of the bishop. But by degrees the rights of the founders began to be asserted: "Ne presbyter territorii alieni sine conscientia sui episcopi in alterius civitatis territorio

[1] Cod. Theodos, XVI, 2, 33; V, 8, 30.
[2] Counc. Orange, A. D. 441, c. 10. Labbe, Concilia, III, p. 1449.
[3] Just. Nov. 123, c. 18, A. D. 546.

praesumat *baselicis aut oratoriis* observare, nisi forte episcopus suus illum cedat episcopo illi in cujus territorio habitare disposuit.[4] Yet the patrons, as can be realized, have to comply with the bishop's regulations before choosing an encumbent for their foundation. In 541 in France a Council of Orleans recognizes the right of presentation. "Let not proprietors introduce into their domain stranger-clerics without the consent of the bishop to whom pertains the government of the Church." And then the parish was to be given only to those in his locality who had made proof of their fitness and "had been given by the bishop permission to exercise the ministry there." This text does not give the right of patronage; it accepts and regulates it. It shows us that it is no longer exercised only by the Bishop-Founder, or Layman-Founder himself, but also by the proprietor who succeeds him. It became at the same time both general and hereditary. The Church submits to it but lays down the conditions under which it is to be exercised. As has already been seen, the cleric must be finally chosen by the bishop in the diocese, examined by him, ordained and instituted by his hands. Patronage made a second step when "villae" were made into dioceses, although in allowing parishes to be established in the *"agri privati"* the bishop had no intention of changing the character of his diocese, and still less of weakening the bonds that united the Church and the city.[5]

---

[4] Conc. Epaon, can. 15, A. D. 515, Migne G. H. Concilia Aevi Merovingici. This refers to bishop-founders; Cf. Hefele, A History of the Councils of the Church, II, p. 663.

[5] Cf. Godfrey, Right of Patronage.

CHAPTER IX

Endowed Churches After Seventh Century; Origin of City Parishes; Difficulties of Patronage

I

By the end of the seventh century the office of parish priest and even the parish system possessed all the essential elements practically, that are found in the pastor and parish at present. Henceforth it remained only to define certain details with greater precision, and to adapt the discipline to the varying needs of the Church, and to extend it to all the sufficiently developed communities.

The right of patronage naturally developed into the organization of benefices [1] though the bishop's authority at times in appointments was somewhat harassed by the patron. The system of patronage is an outgrowth of feudalism, as has been remarked. Smith says that the thing and the name belong to the Frankish domain, and to the period of the Carolingians, for at that time the Church had become the greatest landowner in Gaul. It has been computed that a third of all the real property in Gaul belonged to it.[2] From time to time laymen had been allowed to have the usufruct of some land on condition of paying an annual rent to the churches to which they severally belonged. In the troubled time of Charles Martel and his sons, this use of Church property became almost a necessity of the state. It was not long, however, before the ecclesiastical duties, for the performance of which the lands had originally been intended to provide, were regarded as subordinate to the general privilege of the ownership of the land.

---

[1] For the question of Parochial Benefices cf., Golden, Parochial Benefices in New Code; and L. M. Murray, New Parochial Status in United States.

[2] Roth, Geschichte des Beneficial-Wesens, Erlangen 1850, p. 248, seqq. cf. Smith, Dictionary of Christian Antiquities, Art. Patron.

II

In the eleventh century the larger cities, therefore, witnessed a further development of a parochial system. But the episcopal cities frequently had only one parish in a canonical sense, namely, the cathedral, and this was assigned to a cathedral chapter. The Council of Trent (1563) as shall be seen, went much further and insisted on the strict organization of parishes, even in cities.[3] This was the law of the Church and is the legislation of the present code.

Somewhat earlier than the eleventh, in the eighth century, to be exact, a great many oratories or chapels had been changed into real parish churches. The bishop of the diocese, usually with the cooperation of the temporal rulers, assigned the boundaries of every parish. Thus, in what might be called a "synodus mixta" held in 772 under Tissilo of Bavaria it was decided that the bishop should designate clearly how many and which villages, towns or hamlets each parish priest should govern.[4]

As long as there has been no division into smaller districts the bishop was considered the pastor of the whole diocese, and exercised jurisdiction over it. By the act of ordination a person was incorporated into the diocesan clergy and put on the roster, "matricula" of the diocese. No priest was allowed to serve at a church or oratory in another diocese unless the ordinary for whose diocese he had been ordained had ceded him to the other bishop.[5] The bishop was free to appoint to a rural church any one who had received sacerdotal ordination. Although a synod of Tarragona, A. D. 516, apparently admits a deacon to hold services one week alternately with a priest,[6] yet the mere fact that priests and deacons are mentioned suffices to establish the rule later generally adhered to, that only priests are allowed to function as pastors, for the cleric in higher Orders would naturally be in charge. To prevent nepotism some synods forbade bishops to appoint relatives or favorites to the pastoral office.[7]

---

[3] Counc. Trent, Sess. 24, ch. 13, De Ref.

[4] Hefele, C. G. III, p. 577; Migne P. L., 97, 523, 710.

[5] Synod of Epaon A. D. 517 can. 5, cf. Hefele, vol. 2, p. 663.

[6] Hefele, vol. 2, p. 657.

[7] Synod of Doin, A. D. 527, can. 12. Hefele, vol. 2, p. 698.

III

The free collation of parishes was evercised by the bishop over churches which he had founded from his own revenue. But, as we have seen, the feudal lords who had established rural parishes and endowed them, claimed a share in the appointment, for these churches, according to the Germanic point of view, were the property of the landowners. They claimed the *juspatronatus,* or advowson in view of the fact that a bishop who had founded a church in a diocese not his own, claimed the right to present a clergyman to that church.[8]

In course of time the right of presentation as admitted by the Church was often and flagrantly abused, and developed into lay investitures, which caused the famous struggle between the Teutonic emperors of the eleventh and twelfth centuries, and the Church. The bishops were, furthermore, restricted in their free appointments by the cooperation of the parishoners, who asserted not only a right in the election of bishops, but also in the choice of priests. The principle announced by Hincmar of Rheims: "Ab omnibus debet eligi, qui ab omnibus debet obediri," was logically applied to the selection of pastors. At the same time the Church made repeated laws in order to regulate the exercise of this privilege. Therefore in synodal acts from the ninth century onward it is stated that pastors should be appointed by the bishop or the archdeacon, or the vicar general acting in his name, with the harmonious cooperation of the clergy and the people concerned.[9] This custom prevailed in Italy, and elsewhere, and the Magister Gratianus received it into his decree, and it has been more or less safeguarded in the recent Code.[10] The present legislation on the contrary says that the appointments to the parochial office are to be made by the ordinary (bishop, vicar or prefect apostolic, etc.), or under certain circumstances by the vicar general or administrator.

Presentation has played a much more important and lasting part in the appointment of the Church than was realized when

[8] Synod of Orange, A. D. 441, can. 10, Hefele, vol. 2, p. 276. This is perhaps the oldest document of *juspatronatus.*

[9] Synod of Rome (826) can. 8. A synod of Pavia (855). Cf. Mansi Coll. XV, 17.

[10] C. 20, Dist. XX; cf. can. 455, §1 of Code.

it was first permitted. The Church granted it to founders or benefactors, but this privilege was transmitted, exchanged and extended in various ways, particularly under the feudal system, so that the majority of parishes thus came to depend on patrons. In the diocese of Paris, for example, in the twelfth century, the bishop had the free appointment to only two hundred and fifteen out of four hundred and sixty-nine parishes. At the end of the tenth century, Raimond, Count of Rouerque, exercised the right of patronage over sixty churches and chapels.[11] The Church does not now grant the right of patronage any longer, and even invites those in possession to renounce it without, however, obliging them to do so, recommending rather to respect it as well as the existing right of election.[12]

It is impossible within the limits of this present paper, to enter more in detail into the intricate question of the precise period at which, in the several parts of Christendom, the authority of the bishop of the principal church of a district came to extend over all the villages and towns which were included in that district. That authority was not established without many struggles, and its nature seems to have varied as widely as the extent to which it was recognized. But it came at length to consist in three particulars: 1—The appointments of clerics to parochial or other churches were subject to the bishop's approval. 2—Clerics so appointed were subject to the bishop's jurisdiction, which was exercised partly in the course of annual visitations of the several parishes, partly by requiring the clerics to repair periodically to the bishop's church, for the purpose of being examined. 3—The bishop had the sole right of consecrating churches and altars.

Most authors who have written on this subject bring the history up to the actual establishment of parishes in the eleventh century and allow us to infer that from then on they developed very rapidly and very much along the lines already sketched.[13] The first exact legislation they mention after this time, is that of the Council of Trent in the sixteenth century. In the interim, the parish organization and consequently the appointment was much affected by the development of benefices, for then the

[11] Lesetre, La Paroisse, pp. 64 to 66.
[12] Canons 1450, 1451.
[13] Bouix, Pars. I, Cap. v, Sec. III.

question of irremovability or stability in office came up. To safeguard this, legislation was brought forward, which affected only indirectly the matter of appointment. Before this time, though stability had been desired by the Church it was never properly achieved. Yet by the eleventh century it was an acknowledged fact—that pastors could not be removed—so that greater care was to be exercised in their selection.

Innocent III [14] in IV Council of Lateran 1215, speaks explicitly of the matter. After him Boniface VIII goes onto define specifically the fact in regard to parishes attached to monasteries, and this legislation, it is stated by some, can be applied to other parishes. It is an acknowledged fact that thitherto free collation was exercised by the bishop over all churches founded from his own revenues. After the eleventh, and still more after the twelfth century, the conservative spirit of the Church asserted itself in favor of the integrity of existing benefices.[15]

---

[14] For a more detailed account of this matter, one can consult with profit: Concilium, Cabilonense 813, Can. 42, Mansi XIV, 102; Concilium Papiense, 855, Can. 5, Mon. Ger. Hist. Capitalaria II, 82 ed. Boretius et Krans; Synod Nemausense, 1096, Can. 9, Mansi XX 936; Conc. Londoniense, 1125, Can. 9, Mansi XXI, 332; Synod Remenses 1135, Can. 9, Mansi XXI 460. Also Conc. Lateranense II, 1139, Can. 10, Mansi XXI 529; Claeys-Bouaert, De Can. Cleri Saec. Obed. 294.

[15] C. 3, X, de ecclesiis aedificandis vel reparandis, III, 48.

CHAPTER X

Legislation of Council of Trent

To go forward to the sixteenth century, the immediate origin of the present system presents itself, and historically for this country, this is an important period of legislation. In the time of the Council of Trent there still existed in already ancient dioceses strange to say, cities and country places, where some parochial churches did not have any fixed boundaries, nor the rectors, a flock of their own to govern. Consequently parish priests administered the Sacraments to all that desired them indiscriminately. Not that there had not been attempts to rectify this condition, for as has just been pointed out, there had been. Evidently such efforts failed, otherwise the Council would not have had to emphasize its rulings on the point. The Ecumenical Council enjoined on the bishops for the greater security of the salvation of souls committed to their charge that they divide the people into distinct and well defined parishes, and assign to each parish its own peculiar and perpetual parish priest, who may know his own parishioners and from whom alone they may lawfully receive the Sacraments, otherwise, they were to make such other provisions as may be more beneficial to the character of the place. They were to have the same things done in the cities and other places where no parish church existed, "any customs and privileges, even though immemorial to the contrary notwithstanding." [1]

The Council of Trent, in Session XXIV, *de ref.* cap. 18, gives in detail the manner in which the appointment of pastors is to be made. In general for benefices it is to be made by concursus.[2] The idea of the concursus is to see that the best man gets the best place, and that the unfit do not obtain an office which they cannot properly fulfil. The Council of Trent proposes that an

---

[1] Sess. XXIV, cap. 14, de ref.

[2] Cf. Sess. VII, cap. 13, de ref.

examination be held for all vacant parishes. So clear is the wording of the Council, that the text itself may be given: "The bishop, and he who has the right of patronage, shall nominate in the presence of those who shall be deputed as examiners, certain clerics as capable of governing the vacant church. It shall, nevertheless, be free for others, also, who know any that are fit for the office to give their names in order that a diligent scrutiny may be made as to the age, morals and sufficiency of each, and if the bishop or the provincial synod shall, considering the custom of the country, judge this more expedient, those who may wish to be examined, may be summoned by a public edict. When the time appointed has expired, all those whose names have been entered shall be examined by the bishop, or if he be hindered by his vicar general and by the other examiners who shall be not less than three; to whose votes if they should be equal, or given to distinct individuals, the bishop, or his vicar general may add theirs in favor of whomsoever they shall think most fit.

"As to the examiners, six at least, shall be annually proposed by the bishop or his vicar general in the diocesan synod, who shall be such as to satisfy and to be approved by the said synod. And upon any vacancy occurring in any church the bishop shall elect three out of that number to make the examination with him, and afterwards upon another vacancy following he shall elect out of the six aforesaid the same or other three whom he may prefer. But the said examiners shall be masters or doctors or licentiates in theology or canon law, or such other cleric whether regulars,—even in the order of mendicants,—or seculars as shall seem best adapted thereunto; and they shall all swear on the holy Gospels of God, that they will, setting aside every human affection, faithfully perform their duty. And they shall beware of receiving anything whatsoever, either before or after, on account of this examination; otherwise both the receivers and the givers will incur the guilt of simony, from which they shall not be capable of being absolved until they have resigned the benefice which they had possessed in any manner whatsoever, even before this act; and they shall be rendered incapable of any others for the time to come. And in regard to all these matters, they shall be bound to render an account, not only to God, but also if need be, to the provincial synod, which shall have power to punish them severely, at its own discretion, if it be ascertained that they have done anything contrary to their duty. Then after the examination is completed, a report shall be made of all those who shall have been judged, by the said examiners, fit, by age, morals, learning, prudence and other suitable qualifications, to govern the vacant church. And out of these the bishop shall select him whom he shall judge most fit of all, and to him and to none other shall the church be collated by him unto whom it belongs to collate thereunto.

"But if the church be under the ecclesiastical patronage, and the institution thereunto belongs to the bishop, and to none else, whomsoever the patron shall find most worthy from among those who have been approved of by the examiners, him he shall be bound to present to the bishop, that he may receive institution from him, and when the institution is to proceed from any other than the bishop, then the bishop shall select the worthiest from among the worthy, and him the patron shall present to him unto whom the institution belongs.

"But if it be under lay patronage, the individual who shall be presented by the patron, must be examined by the bishop, unless he be already found fit. And in all the above mentioned cases to none other, but to one of those who have been examined as aforesaid, and have been approved of by the examiners, according to the rule prescribed above, shall the church be committed, nor shall any devolution, or appeal, interposed even before the Apostolic See, or the legate, or vice-legate or nuncio of that see, or before any bishops, or metropolitans, or primates, or patriarchs, hinder or suspend the report of the aforesaid examiners, from being carried into execution; for the rest the vicar whom the bishop has, at his own discretion, already deputed for the time being to the church that is vacant, or he may afterwards happen to depute thereunto, shall be removed from the charge and administration of the said church, until it be provided for, either by the appointment of the vicar himself, or of some other person, who has been approved of, and elected as above; and all provisions and institutions made otherwise than according to the above mentioned form, shall be accounted surreptitious; any exemptions, indults, privileges, preventions, appropriations, new provisions, indults granted to any university whatsoever for a certain sum, and any other impediments whatsoever in opposition to this decree notwithstanding.

"If, however, the said parish church should possess so slight a revenue as not to allow of the trouble of all this examination, or should no one seek to undergo this examination; or if by any reason of the open factions or dissensions which are met with in some places, more grievous quarrels and tumults may easily be excited thereby; the ordinary, may, omitting the formality, have recourse to a private examination if, in his conscience, with the advice of the examiners deputed, he shall judge this expedient, observing however, the other things as prescribed above. It shall also be lawful for the provincial synod, if it shall judge that there be any particulars that ought to be added to, or retrenched from, the above regulations concerning the form of examination, to provide accordingly." [3]

This legislation marks a tremendous progress in the manner of appointing to the parochial office. It is an evidence, too, that the evolution of the matter of the appointment of pastors to churches has been along safe and healthy lines. For this was the result. Yet as excellent as this declaration of the Council of Trent seems by contrast with the previous ruling, there was still much to be desired. And so it was left to the succeeding Popes to complete and amplify the procedure, and to define more exactly certain details. The conditions, the subject matter, and the method of this concursus examination were perfected by Popes Pius V,[4] Clement XI,[5] and Benedict XIV.[6] These took up the work where the Fathers of the Council left off, for it became necessary to set forth more clearly the manner of procedure. The wording of the council's decree was vague enough to be subjected to various interpretations, and therefore in order to obviate anything like confusion in its application, many points had to be further clarified. The popes have already been mentioned, in their encyclicals and constitutions laid down the fol-

[3] Sess. XXIV, cap. 18, de ref.

[4] Const. "In Conferendis," March 18, 1567, Fontes 119; and "Apostalatus Officium," August 19, 1567; Bull. Taur.; VII, pp. 555, 605; Cf. Wernz-Vidal, Jus. Cannonicum, II, p. 772.

[5] Clement XI, Encyclical "Quo Parochiales," Jan. 10, 1721. Cf. A.S.S., VII, p. 353 seqq.

[6] Benedict XIV, Const. "Cum Illud," Dec. 14, 1742. Codex Juris Canonici, Rome, 1919, Docum. IV, p. 807.

lowing definite rules: 1—The bishop when he receives notice of the vacancy of a parish, should immediately appoint a suitable administrator who should hold the place during the interregnum. 2—Then a public notice should be given of the concursus to be held, and a suitable time set during which all the names and documents and information of the competitors should be given to the chancellor. 3—The examination should embrace not only the candidate's knowledge, but also his age, his morals, his past services, and his ability and the qualities which may fit him for the vacant office. 4—After the examination the synodal examiners are to give the findings and the vote, to the bishop who himself was to choose the most fit. 5—If any candidate appealed from the concursus because of the examiners or the judgment of the bishop, the whole proceedings were to be repeated before the judge of appeal. In case the See was impeded, the vicar general, or during the vacancy of the See the administrator could send out the notice of the concursus. But who could take part in this concursus? All priests of the diocese and even those outside the diocese who were engaged in parish work, unless the common law of the Church forbade them to do so. Naturally a diocesan priest had preference over an outsider. There were some who felt that an outsider should not be allowed to compete in the examination at all unless the priests of the diocese did not care to.

This form of appointment applied through the concursus to all parochial benefices canonically instituted, which were perpetual, unless they were exempt by the law or by some special privileges. Those who were appointed to other charges did not receive their appointment in this way, such as those parishes connected with a monastery or with a cathedral chapter. Nor did it embrace those which were movable "ad nutum ordinarii." *"Pro ipso vero parocho amovibili examinando, non tenetur ordinarius uti examinatoribus synodalibus, sed uti potest quibus ipse maluerit; nec pariter fieri debet concursus."* [7]

Parishes in charge of religious or united to some dignity or chapter of canons did not strictly come under this ruling. To all the *"concurrentes"* in the concursus were to be assigned the

---

[7] S. C. C. Jan. 12, 1619. Thesaurus Resolutionum Sacrae Congregationis Concilii.

same questions, viz., the same case in moral theology, and the same text of the Gospel on which to write a homily. The questions were to be answered and the case to be solved by all at the same time, and also the homily to be written simultaneously. All were to be allowed the same length of time. The examination was to be in writing, and all competitors must be examined in the same room. No one could leave during the written examinations, nor could an outsider be admitted into the examination room until the papers had been handed in. The answers must be written in Latin. The homily alone was to be written in the vernacular, and all the writing must be done by hand. After the papers had been handed in they were to be countersigned by the chancellor, the examiners and the bishop or his vicar. According to the Constitution of Pius V, *"In Conferendis,"* March 18, 1567, if there was to be an appeal it must be made within ten days. The court of appeal was to be regulated in this manner. From a Suffragan See the appeal was to the Metropolitan. From a Metropolitan See to the designated See or bishop, or it could be made to the Holy See according to circumstances. From the Constitution, *"Cum Illud,"* we have the ruling that no new document could be introduced into the appeal. In all cases appeal was to be *"in devolutivo."*

CHAPTER XI

Early Customs and Legislation in the United States

In our own United States in the beginning, because owing to the extent of the first dioceses, the small number of priests, and the difficulty of communication, and for many other obstacles, the strict parochial division could not possibly have been introduced. Missionaries often had to consider the possibility and convenience of the people rather than the boundaries of their parishes. By common consent in 1810, bishops of America even found it necessary to grant jurisdiction to one another over their respective territories, and this jurisdiction they were practically forced to communicate to their clergy.[1] The second Provincial Council of Baltimore 1833 was compelled to withdraw this arrangement, as through it many abuses had crept in. (Decree No. 10.)

Owing to the rather confused state of affairs, because of the vicissitudes under which church organizations labored in this country at that time, it often happened that several priests claimed as their own the same district and the same church, and exercised authority therein independently one of the other. That such a state of things was contrary to the tradition of the Church and good government, the first Provincial Council of Baltimore in 1829 stated somewhat emphatically.[2] It was besides the source of great confusion and much discord, and so the Council felt called upon to oblige bishops to correct such disorders as soon as possible, by putting one pastor in charge of each place with other priests to assist him if necessary.

In 1866 the fathers of the second Plenary Council of Baltimore, having in mind the great advantage of parochial organiza-

---

[1] 1st Prov. Synod 1810, Art. I, Ecclesiastical Discipline.

[2] Cf. II Plen. Counc. 1866 & 1st Plen. Counc. of Balto., Dec. 4, 1852. When there was more than one who claimed to be pastor of same parish, the first appointed was to be pastor and the others his assistants. N. 111-112.

tion, such as the common law of the Church required, and as it existed universally in Catholic countries, and knowing full well that circumstances would not allow them to establish this regime in their own country immediately, made an effort to introduce it gradually. Therefore, they made the declaration that in every diocese, a certain district, equivalent to a parish, with well defined limits, should be assigned to each church, and that to its rector, parochial, or quasi-parochial rights should be given. They were careful to draw attention to the fact that in the use of the names, parochial rights, parish and parish priest, they wished to indicate in no way that they were bestowing upon the rectors of any church whatsoever the right of irremovability.[3] This meant merely the erection of quasi-parishes in the full canonical sense of the term. The rectors of such parishes did not acquire the standing of canonical pastors and hence their jurisdiction remained simply delegated and was not ordinary as that of a canonical pastor today. From that time on the pastors in this country, since there were only *quasi-parishes,* exercised the care of souls, not in their own name, but in that of the bishop. The question then arose as to the method to be pursued in the appointment of pastors here in the United States. The discipline of the second and third Plenary Councils of Baltimore prescribed an examination for the office. Each candidate was to make an examination before the bishop and two priests selected by the bishop. Moreover, no one could be a candidate unless he labored in the diocese on the missions for at least five years previous. If one were not in the diocese for five years, he could be only an administrator; after five years he had to take the examination and then he was made real pastor. Regulars who lived in these provinces were not bound by this legislation.[4]

The Third Plenary Council of Baltimore went further than this and prescribed the "*concursus*" of the Council of Trent for those candidates who sought an irremovable rectorship. It was this council which first established the irremovable or permanent rectorships. Bishops were recommended to make one-tenth [5] of

[3] Second Plenary Counc. of Baltimore, 1866, n. 120-125.

[4] II Plen. Counc. Balt. Acta et Decreta Tit III §126, pp. 79-80.

[5] III. Plen. Counc. Balt. Acta et Decreta Tit. II. Cap. V, n. 33. Cf. Golden's Parochial Benefices, p. 99. "This number could not be increased by the Bishops for twenty years after the promulgation of the Council.

all the parishes in their dioceses, irremovable in this sense. As the Fathers of the Council said: *"Volumus tamen, ut Episcopi facultate gaudeant, pro prima vice, omisso concursu, rectores inamovibiles designandi quos magis dignos et idoneos coram Deo judicaverint, praehabito consilio Consultorum suorum."* [6] Consequently the bishops could choose the first irremovable rector without any concursus as long as they heard the Consultors. But thereafter, all candidates for such a rectorship had to pass a concursus. One other exception was made here, i.e., that the concursus could be waived in favor of an ecclesiastic, whose learning was well know or whose services to the Church were worthy of special consideration in the eyes of the Bishop after hearing the opinion of the Examiners.[7] Canon 459 §4, of the Code, requires that as far as the United States is concerned, concursus for irremovable rectorship is to be held, *"donec Sedes Apostolica aliud decreverit."* [8]

The method to be used for the concursus is defined in the acts of the Third Council and its decrees. It is substantially the same as that prescribed by the Council of Trent and more fully determined by the Constitution of Benedict XIV. Several minor changes were introduced to accommodate it to the state of affairs found here in the United States.

One of the conditions laid down by the Fathers was that only such candidates would be allowed to take the examination as were of good morals, had exercised the ministry successfully within the diocese for at least ten years or had otherwise given signs of their ability to govern a parish with success, or had been a simple rector for three years.[9] It would be well to give briefly an outline of the particular legislation of this council on the concursus. 1—The concursus for an irremovable rectorship

---

Nor did the Council intend that either the removable or the irremovable rectors be canonical pastors, but hoped to approach this discipline little by little as circumstances would allow. There was, on the part of Rome, the intention that canonical parishes should be erected by this Council, but after hearing the Ordinaries, Rome decided that the missionary status could be tolerated. It is plainly evident from the consideration of this Council that the Church was making rapid strides toward the common law ideal."

[6] III. Plen Counc. Balt. Acta et Decreta Tit. II. §7, p. 23.

[7] III. Plen. Counc. Balt. Acta et Decreta Tit. II. §57, p. 57-58.

[8] Can. 459 §4.

[9] III Plen. Counc. Balt. l. c. n. 43.

must be made before the bishop or his vicar general and at least three examiners, who are to be chosen from among these constituted like synodal and prosynodal examiners (according to Cap. 3 of III Plen. Counc. of Balt.). There must always be at least three examiners unless this number cannot be had on account of the small number of priests within the diocese.[10] 2—When a mission enjoying the right of irremovability becomes vacant, this fact is to be made known to the clergy of the diocese by the bishop. At the same time he is to tell them that a competitive examination will be held for that place. At least ten days' time should be allowed, so that those who wish to enter this concursus, could indicate their intention and ask permission of the bishop to compete. At the same time testimonials or documents concerning their qualities and fitness should be sent into the chancellor of the diocese, or to the person designated by the bishop.[11] The limit of ten days may be extended to twenty days by order of the bishop. According to the decree of the Sacred Cong. of the Propagation of the Faith, our bishops received faculties to extend this time to thirty complete days on account of "dioecesium amplitudinis, sive locorum distantiae, sive gravissimorum negotiorum, quae assiduam episcoporum solicitudinem exigent."[12] After the time set by the bishop had passed no more papers should be received. The bishop is then to decide who shall be allowed to enter the concursus.[13]

The examination "de scientia" is to be held both in writing and orally. Questions are to be given in Moral Theology and Dogma, in Liturgy and Canon Law, and should take up such parts as are (more) necessary and ought to be known. A question or two from the Catechism should also be given in order to find out with what skill the candidate can explain Christian doctrine, and to ascertain the method he follows.[14] 4—In order that none of the candidates should hope to pass without the necessary knowledge of what is supposed to be known, the examiners are to be told to do their duty with religious exactness.[15]

---

[10] III Plen. Counc. Balt. l. c. n. 42.
[11] III Plen. Counc. Balt. l. c. n. 51.
[12] Acta et Decreta III, Plen. Counc. Balt., p. CIII.
[13] III Plen. Counc. Balt. l. c. n. 42-43.
[14] III Plen. Counc. Balt. l. c. n. 44.
[15] III Plen. Counc. Balt. l. c. n. 46.

5—No one is to retire before the test is completed, except in case of necessity.[16] 6—The Bible, the Council of Trent, and the Corpus Juris Canonici, together with a concordance, are the only books allowed as helps to the competitors. All other books or pamphlets are prohibited. If any one is caught cheating, he shall be expelled and excluded from further competition.[17] 7—The oral examination cannot be held unless the bishop or his substitute and at least three examiners are present.[18] 8—The examiners must weigh carefully the practical knowledge of each candidate as shown in his explanation of Christian doctrine as well as his skill in adapting himself to the mental capacity of the young. In the written examination they must also consider the opinions of the different competitors, their use of suitable words as well as the perspicuity and beauty of language in the sermons.[19] 9—Consideration must be taken not only of the learning of the candidates but also of the other qualities required in a successful parish priest, and so the Fathers of the Council thought it wise to embody the following decree: *"Probe igitur advertant examinatores, accurato examine sibi inquirendum esse, non solum de concurrentium scientia ac doctrina; sed eandem, immo forte majorem conferendam esse industriam in alias perscrutandas dotes animarum regimimi consentaneas. Ne igitur gravi suo muneri desint, literarum peritiae scrutinio minime neglecto, diligenter inquirant de ceteris qualitatibus regendae ecclesiae necessariis de aetate scilicet, de anteactae vitae ratione, muniis antea exercitis, gravitate et honestate morum, prudentia, temporalium rerum administrandarum peritia, obsequiis Ecclesiae hactenus praestitis; qui demum tales sint ut oves suas verbo et exemplo pascere queant."* [20] Information regarding these qualities can be taken from the papers sent in by the candidates before the examination as well as from other reliable sources.[21] 10—The examiners are not competent to select the pastor, nor should they even pass judgment as to which of all the candidates is most fit. All they are required and allowed to do is to decide

[16] III Plen. Counc. Balt. l. c. n. 47

[17] III Plen. Counc. Balt. l. c. n. 48.

[18] III Plen. Counc. Balt. n. 49.

[19] III Plen. Counc. of Balt. n. 50.

[20] III Plen. Counc. of Balt. n. 51.

[21] III Plen. Counc. of Balt. n. 31.

who among these competitors are fit for the office in question and report the names of such to the bishop. The bishop alone then chooses *"quem ipse digniorem in Domino censuerit."* But he can take counsel with the examiners before his selection is made.[22] 11—Judgment as to the fitness of the candidates must be made by the examiners before they leave the place of examination, and separately from the bishop or his substitute. This judgment may be passed by means of a secret ballot or openly "...... congruentius tamen videtur, ut examinatores inter se suffragia communicent, quo ad acta referri possit, qui probati, qui non probati fuerint.[23] 12—The bishop or his substitute has no vote in the judgment of the examiners unless the ballots are evenly divided, or in case of "vota singularia." In such cases then the bishop's vote is the decisive one and must be made known to the examiners before their departure, since this pertains to the completion of the examination. In this manner judgment is passed upon each and every candidate and they are found fit or unfit. Suspension of judgment is not allowed.[24] 13—After the examiners have passed their judgment, the parish in question must be given to one of those found capable.[25] 14—In case the bishop alone knows of some certain defects in one or other of the candidates and this defect is sufficient to render him unworthy, he may pass over such a person and select another.[26]

The Constitution of Benedict XIV, "Cum Illud" §6 says: "Whenever the bishop passes over one man and grants the office to another for reasons known to himself alone, he should notify the judge of appeals of this reason when one of the others makes an appeal. This should be done by a personal secret letter to the judge and the latter is then held to the seal of secrecy in regard to this matter. If the bishop suspects the judge of appeals, the reason need not be sent to him but preferably to the Prefect of the S. Congregation of the Council. This also must be done by secret letter. If the judge of appeals decides in favor of the bishop's choice, no further appeal can be had. If on the contrary he decides against the bishop, the priest who received the office

---

[22] III Plen. Counc. of Balt. n. 32.
[23] III Plen. Counc. of Balt. n. 53.
[24] III Plen. Counc. of Balt. n. 54.
[25] III Plen. Counc. of Balt. n. 55.
[26] III Plen. Counc. of Balt. n. 56.

has the right of appealing to another judge, retaining in the meantime the parish obtained through the concursus. The sentence of this second judge is final. If the present incumbent of the office receives a favorable sentence the case is settled and he retains his position. If the second judge also decides against the bishop's choice, the election is null."

Besides this legislation regarding the particular concursus the Acts and Decrees of the III Plen. Council of Baltimore also contained certain rulings in regard to the general concursus. The general concursus differs from the particular or special in this, that the examination "de scientia" is to be held at a stated time each year, whether there is any vacancy at that time or not. The standing of the candidates is determined here in reference to "doctrina" and preserved for future use. The other qualities are not examined until a vacancy occurs. All those passing the test "de doctrina" are considered fit subjects in that regard for any rectorship within the next six years. If they desire to be candidates for such positions again after this time, then they must make another concursus. This form, called the general concursus, is to be used only when the diocese is confronted with such circumstances as make it very hard to hold the particular concursus whenever an irremovable pastorate falls vacant. Some bishops prefer this form of concursus and perhaps some day it may become the common law of the Church.[27] This, however, makes little difference in the standing of the quasi-parishes, and quasi-pastors before church law. When in 1908 the dioceses of the United States were taken away from the jurisdiction of the Congregation of the Propaganda, and put under the government of the common law of the Church, the existing legislation in this country for pastors was in no way changed. The Consistorial Congregation declared likewise on June 28, 1915, that the decree of Pius X, "Maxima Cura," August 20, 1910, had not given greater permanency to the movable pastors of parishes in the United States. They still remained the vicars of the ordinaries. The publication of the Code in 1918, had quite a different effect, and under the present law the divisions of the dioceses constitute parishes in the full sense of the term, and the priests in charge of them have all the duties and rights of canonical pastors.

[27] Cf. III Plen. Council of Baltimore, l. c. §50, p. 30.

For those countries outside of the United States, there is every reason to believe that they followed the common law of the Church as laid down by the Council of Trent, and the popes that have already been mentioned, since that time. There is, however, a petition addressed to the Fathers of the Vatican Council of 1870, which throws some light at least on the condition of affairs in this regard in certain countries. As the Council of the Vatican, by no means, completed its full program, practically all the disciplinary measures proposed were never acted upon, and this question, along with many others, was never considered.

The petition [28] was a two-fold one, as set forth in the preparatory acts of the Council as published by Bishop Martin of Paderborn. It concerns itself mostly about lay patronage, of which at all times, it might be said, there has been an abuse much to the prejudice of parishes and immortal souls. The bishops who drew up this petition proposed that the council make wise measures to prevent further difficulties and inconveniences. The suggestion was made that the patron be limited to choosing one of three priests proposed to him by the ordinary.

The second proposition is about the concursus for vacant parishes prescribed by the Council of Trent. The remark is made that the requirements of this concursus seem to be no longer in harmony with actual circumstances in most of the dioceses; and that besides, in many dioceses, a special concursus, such as the decree of the Council calls for, no longer takes place, owing to the number of difficulties it entails. Furthermore in a number of dioceses, the Holy See has granted that in place of this special concursus, which should take place for each vacant parish in particular, that a general concursus be substituted. That is to say, that each year an examination be undergone by the priests of the diocese to give them a kind of classification in regard to their aptitude and merits in the pastoral ministry. The fact that propositions of this kind were found to be agreeable to the bishops of other countries, the writer of the petition claims, showed that the decree of the Council of Trent should be modified in a manner more in con-

[28] Les Travaux du Concil du Vatican—Par Monseigneur Conrad Martin Eugene de Paderborn—Paris 1873, p. 131.

formity with the conditions that are met with actually in most dioceses, and that as the conditions of the dioceses of the different countries are rather different, it should be left to the conscience of each bishop to choose the kind of concursus he wishes to have in his own diocese. It is maintained that such an examination would correspond to the moral dignity, as well as the zeal for souls, pastoral prudence, and scientific aptitude of the priests. As no action could be taken in this matter by the Council of the Vatican, the manner of appointment of pastors for the dioceses of different countries was left, in general, as it had been before the time of the Council.

CHAPTER XII

HISTORICAL SUMMARY:

CANDIDATE; ONE WHO APPOINTS; FREE COLLATION, ELECTION, PRESENTATION, RESERVATIONS

By a brief review the main points in our short consideration of the appointments of parish priests may be summed up. The chief requirements are concerned with the age, the orders and character of the man. As to the age of those who may become pastors, let it be said that, although in providing for ecclesiastical benefices only that age is demanded which of itself is necessary for the discharge of the office in a becoming manner, the Canons of the Church have always specified a required number of years. Thus, in general, in the very old law of the Church, under pain of nullity, the man appointed to the parochial office, must have already begun his twenty-fifth year. This is gathered from the Constitution of Pope Alexander III, in the Latern Council, *"Quia Nonnulli,"* which was later confirmed by Gregory X: *"Licet canon, a felicis recordationis. . . . Alexandro Papa III, praedecessore nostro editus, inter caetera statuerit, ut nullus regimen ecclesiae parochialis suscipiat, nisi vigesimum quintun annum attigerit . . . .*"[1] Before this time, of course, what has already been said, held good, that is, thirty years was the age of ordination and consequently of the pastorate.[2] The Council of Trent simply renewed the ruling of Popes Alexander and Gregory: *"Inferiora beneficia ecclesiastica, praesertim curam animarum habentia, personis dignis . . . juxta constitutionem Alexandri III et Gregorii X . . . editam, conferatum aliter autem facta collatio sive provisio, omnino irritetur."*[3] In

[1] Cap. *"Licet,"* Tit. 6, Lib. 1 in 6. C I, *de electione et electi potestate,* 6, I, in VI°.

[2] Cf. Imbart de la Tour, p. 127 seqq. on p. 136, n. 2, *Capit. a Sacerdotibus proposita,* c. 17.

[3] Sess. 6, *De Ref.* Cap.

the present law one must be a priest and according to it the priesthood is not given before the completion of the twenty-fourth year.

On the question of orders, we know that as a rule in ancient ecclesiastical law offices and benefices were reserved to clerics.[4] When a parish priest was concerned, the choice could fall on some one who was already an ordained priest,[5] or even on one who was only tonsured or in any other order below the priesthood provided he received the priesthood within a year from the date that he took office. According to a decretal of Pope Boniface VIII (1294-1303) it is evident that no sacred orders were necessary.[6] Moreover, some authors assert that not even minor orders were demanded as a necessity for the validity of the appointment. Thus Fagnamus says: *"Nam parochiales (ecclesiae) conferuntur etiam clerics primae tonsurae.*[7] All that was necessary in such cases was that the appointed one be ordained to the priesthood within a short time, i.e., one year.[8] The Council of Trent did not make any change in this regard and so, even after this time the sacerdotal character was not a necessary requisite for the validity of the appointment. Now, however, there can be no question about this.

The character was always a very serious consideration in the candidates for the parochial office. *"Ministeria quae curam animarum habent adnexam, nullus omnino suscipiat . . . nisi scientia et moribus commendatus existat."* [9] Consequently all

---

[4] C. 12, X. De Elect. VII, 5; c. 15, *de electione et electi potestate,* I, 6, in VI.

[5] Cap. 7, §2, X, *De Elect.,* I, 6.

[6] Cap. 8, De Praebend. III, 4, in VI, and Cap. II, de Inst. III, 4, in VI, ubi severitatis temperatur capitis V, X, I, 14, cum requirebatur subdiaconatus vel dispensatur ab episcopo, ordines minores, dummodo promovendus talibus versaretur conditionibus, ut posset breve intra tempus, presbyteratus ordinem suscipere. Cap. 14, 35, De Elect. in VI; Cap. II, De Aet. 1, 6, in Clem.; Counc. Trid. Sess. XXIV, Cap. 12, de ref., Gasparri, De Sacra Ordinatione, n. 655 seqq.

[7] In his chapter *"De Aetate et qualitate,"* 8.

[8] Pirhing, *"Jus Canonicum Nova Methodo explicatum"* "tit" XIV lib. I, decretalium n. 41.

[9] Cf. Can. 154 of Code seems to be based on "Cum in cunctis" 7, De Elect. C. 7, X, de electione et electi potestate, I, 6; C. 14, X, de officio judicis ordinarii, I, 31; C. Trent, Sess. XXI, de ref., C. 6; Sess. XXIV, de ref. C. 18; S. Pius V, "In Conferendis," March 18, 1567; Benedict XIV, Encyc. "Cum Illud," Dec. 14, 1742, §7, 11; S.C.C. Ep. Jan. 10, 1721; S.C. de Prop. Fide instr. (Ad Archiep. Hiberniae) June 25, 1791.

those who were not in good standing or who bore a bad reputation, were ineligible, and if they incurred the guilt of public immorality, they were to be degraded from office, if they already held one. In this class are to be found criminals, infamous, excommunicated, suspended, interdicted, etc.

There is no doubt that in the pastor more than in the ordinary priest must be found, the knowledge necessary for the administration of the sacraments, particularly Penance, also for preaching the Word of God and administering to the spiritual and temporal welfare of the flock. In general, all the theological and ecclesiastical science that pertains to the fruitful care of souls was required. Thus always there was an examination by the bishop to ascertain this and later the concursus prescribed by the Council of Trent was perfected by the other legislative acts we have already mentioned.

There should be but one pastor for each parish. In the old discipline it was sometimes found that several pastors were ruling the same congregation independently of each other. Though the plurality of pastors does not necessarily militate against the essence of the parish office, it does often lead to confusion and conflict. It is not clear when nor how the Church first forbade that there be in one and the same parish more than one pastor, but individual cases are known in which there was a decision that there be only one, in order to avoid further trouble.[10] Likewise the mind of the Church has always been to give but one benefice or parish to one priest.[11]

Lastly, in the act of appointment three stages may be con-

---

[10] Lutetiis Parisiorum, ex. gr. quaedam paroecia a tribus parochis simul antea gubernabatur, et serius a duobus. Quorum circa jus praecedentiae controversias et dubia Sacra Rituum Congregatio, die ii, Dec. 1728, solvit, quin ullo mode ne leviter quidem, innueret existentiam duorum parochorum sacris canonibus esse contrariam. Cf. Rossi-De Paroecia, pp. 82, 83.

[11] Pariter S.C.C. (in casa Sutrina, 16, Junii 1701) haec respondit: *"Licet unicam parochi duo regere valeant ecclesiam* distincti tamen censentur ubi separatim habent gregem." (Giraldi, *Animadversiones et Additiones ad Barbosam, De Officio et Potestate Paroch.* cap. 1, n. 44; et Sacra Congregatio in Tyburtina, 25 Martii, et 9 Junii 1757). C. 3, C. X, qu. 3; c. 20, C. XVI, qu. 7; C. 54, X, de electione et elect. pot. I, 6; I, 28; C. 3, X, De Clericis non residentibus, III, 4; C. 5, 7, 15, 28, X de proeb. et. dig. III, 5; C. I, X de excessibus praelet et Sub. V, 31; C. 3, de Officio Ordinarii, I, 16, in VI; Counc. of Trent, Sess. VII, de ref. C. 4, 5; Sess. XXIV, de ref. C. 17.

sidered, viz., the election of the person, the granting of the title, and the taking possession, which is called installation or investiture. When the nomination is the free choice of the bishop alone,[12] it is called *"libera collatio."* When it is through the presentation of some one such as a patron, or the election as in the case of Concordats, it is called institution. When there is free collation, as was and is the case in this country for the majority of parishes, the bishop can appoint any one at all whom he deems worthy. In those countries as France, Belgium, Spain, and Germany, etc., where Concordats have existed, the government presents to the bishop a candidate for his approval or enjoys the right of alternative collation with the bishop.[13] In this country since the Code of 1918, parishes are considered to be parochial benefices, and the appointment is by means of the concursus.[14] Before that time the parishes of the United States were not held as benefices. However, for many of the benefices elsewhere there is a patron, who has the right to present his candidate. This right usually must be exercised in a specified time. This has been found to be an awkward arrangement, and the Church no longer grants it. Election by popular choice apparently is still practiced in some countries like Switzerland.[15] In all cases the bishop has the right of approval. In the United States the trustees at one time claimed the prerogatives of patrons and even more extensive ones. This gave occasion to the declaration of the first Provincial Council of Baltimore (1829 n. VI) that the American church recognized no right of patronage for any individual or moral person.

There is one point that has not been touched upon in this paper, that is, reservations to the Holy See. It has been passed

---

[12] In this regard there is something of interest in the decrees of the 1st Baltimore Synod 1829-31. The bishops of the U. S. had in their first decree based the movability of pastors on the promise of obedience made by them at the time of their ordination. Propaganda in a general meeting June 28, 1830, corrected the decrees, and June 30, 1831, published the corrected decrees, saying that pastors were movable *"ad nutum"* according to Ben. XIV, not by virtue of the solemn promise of obedience made at ordination. They add that the U. S. bishops could tell their pastors to keep this promise in mind.

[13] Cf. Augustine Comm., vol. II, p. 524.

[14] Cf. Canon 459, §4; cf. C. 14 of this Dissertation.

[15] Cf. Ayrinhac, Const. of Church, p. 319; Pius IX, Const. "Etsi Multa" Nov. 21, 1873, Fontes, 566; Cf. Augustine II, p. 524, first paragraph.

over, because up to the present no trace of it has been found in our country. All concede that the Pope by reason of the plenitude of his powers both of jurisdiction, and administration has the right, strictly speaking to make all or any appointments in the Church that he desires to make. And the popes, particularly, since the Avignon period (1304-1378) had established numerous reservations. Many of them have ceased but some still continue in force. The principal of reservation had been emphatically asserted already in a Decretal of Clement VI.[16] This decretal mentions as reserved to the Roman Pontiff all benefices which became vacant at the Apostolic See. This term is explained by canonists as meaning every benefice becoming vacant where the Pope resided, or within a radius of 40 miles (40,000 paces), was subject to papal reservation. Therefore any benefice whose holder died within that territory could not be conferred by the local Ordinary, but only by the Pope. The law was adopted as a rule of the Apostolic Chancery. But it may be added that neither the law laid down in the decretals, nor the first rule of the Apostolic Chancery was ever applied in this country. Nor could it in justice be applied, for with the exception of a few parishes in the province of San Francisco and in New Orleans, there were no benefices strictly so-called in the United States.[17] Whether it is tenable that papal reservations do not interfere with the bishop's free right of appointing parish priests, is something that will be discussed in a further development of this paper.[18]

---

[16] Cf. c. 2, XIII, 4; concerning historical part. See Scherer, I, 283; Wernz, 1st ed. 11, p. 448 ff.; Sagmuller, p. 272, Bouix, De Parocho, p. 310 ff.

[17] Cf. Cath. Encyc. II 474. Other rules like those concerning papal months in alternative collation refer to higher benefices.

[18] Cf. Can. 1435.

PART II—MODERN LEGISLATION

CHAPTER XIII

The Pastor

Canon 451

§1. Parochus est sacerdos vel persona moralis cui paroecia collata est in titulum cum cura animarum sub Ordinarii loci auctoritate exercenda.

§2. Parochis aequiparantur cum omnibus juribus et obligationibus paroecialibus et parochorum nomine in jure veniunt;

> **1°. Quasi-parochi, qui quasi-paroecias regunt, de quibus in can. 216, §3.**
>
> **2°. Vicarii paroeciales, si plena potestate paroeciáli sint praediti.**

§3. Circa militum cappellanos sive maiores, sive minores, standum peculiaribus Scantae Sedis praescriptis.

I. *Definition of a Secular Pastor*

From this canon one can define a pastor or parish priest as the priest or moral person to whom a parish is entrusted in title, and who must exercise care of souls under the authority of the Ordinary of the place. In this first part consideration shall be given only to the secular pastor so that the moral person may be disregarded for the present as the pastor of parishes united to moral person shall be considered in the second article of this chapter. Be it remarked at the very outset, that this requirement of the priesthood in the appointee to the pastoral office is an innovation in the church's legislation. Not that the pastors before the

Code of 1918 were not priests, but that it was possible for one to be appointed to that office before he had received the Sacred Ordination. And as a matter of fact, there is good reason to believe that this state of affairs did obtain at times in the past.[1]

The office of the *"Parochus"* comprises then three distinct features,[2] viz., first that it must have attached to it the care of souls (this is the end for which it was instituted by the Church); secondly, that it must be exercised in a parish or parish church conferred *"in titulum"* (i. e., in title); thirdly, that in the discharge of his functions and duties, the pastor is always subject to the bishop of the diocese. When the expression secular pastor is used, it signifies an individual physical person who has been raised to the Holy Priesthood, and who is a member of the diocesan clergy. By the expression *"cura animarum,"* is signified the spiritual care of souls. In the Church which is a true spiritual society, instituted by Jesus Christ for the salvation of souls, there is no office or power whose purpose is not the spiritual good of souls. To carry out this work of the eternal welfare of men, the Church grants to the pastor ordinary jurisdiction in the internal forum by common law from the very moment that he is raised to this dignity.[3] His power is ordinary in the sense that it is attached to his office and defined by universal ecclesiastical law. This ordinary jurisdiction does not include the power to reserve sins or censures nor to absolve from reserved cases. Jurisdiction of the internal forum affects primarily and directly the private good of the faithful, while jurisdiction of the external forum refers immediately to the public and common good of the Church, and has juridical and social effects.[4] As the Pastor enjoys no legislative powers, he cannot be said to possess jurisdiction in the external forum at all.

This jurisdiction which he possesses, he may delegate, but

---

[1] A more detailed explanation of this subject will be given in the succeeding chapter of this dissertation.

[2] Cf. Bouix, De Parocho, pars. 1, sec. II, cap. IX.

[3] There is no doubt that the pastor possesses jurisdiction in the internal extra-sacramental forum as well as in the sacramental forum through the administration of the sacraments, and a paternal vigilance over his flock. Cf. Rossi, De Paroecia, p. 67 seq. n. 89; Bouix, De Parocho, pars. 1, sect. II, cap. IX, §2.

[4] Cf. Wernz-Vidal, Jus Canonicum, II, n. 365.

only within those limits set down by law.[5] Thus he may authorize any priest to assist at a particular marriage in his parish, and his assistants to assist at any marriage there.[6] Though a parish priest cannot enact laws or precepts binding in conscience; he may formulate certain rules regarding, for example, the ordering and moderating of divine services, the watching over of the Church, the taking care of and defending its goods. These, however, do not impose a strict obligation; and do not constitute acts of jurisdiction, properly so-called, but rather acts of paternal administration in the nature of advices and practical direction.[7]

For the same reason though in general the pastor cannot dispense from the laws of the Church, yet by special concession of the legislator the Code allows him under certain conditions to dispense from the laws of fasting and abstinence, the sanctification of feasts and also in particular cases from impediments to marriage.[8]

Rossi[9] says most truly that *"certissimum ac verissimum parochi officium"* is to exercise the care of souls over the people living in the part of the diocesan territory which has been assigned to him. In canon 94, can be found a suitable definition of parishioner: *"fidels omnes qui domicilium vel quasi—domicilium, habent in paroecia, nisi sint exempt."* [10] But this means to include not only the Catholics but also the non-Catholics as well, whom the pastor should consider as commended to him in the Lord in order that he might bring about their conversion to the true faith.[11] The word *"parishioner"* is extended here to embrace strangers, *"peregrini,"* and *"vagi,"* who come under the care of the pastor of the place.

The second essential note of the pastor is that the parish in

---

[5] Cf. Canon 199 §1, and Response of Comm. for Authentic Interpretation of Code, Oct. 19, 1919, A. A. S. XI.

[6] A very good discussion on this point which can be consulted with profit, is an article by P. Maroto, published in the *"Apollinaris,"* vol. I, n. 2, p. 104 seq.

[7] Cf. Chelodi, Jus de Personis, n. 233; "(*Parochi*) praeter *ordinariam fori interni,* habent quoque *potestatem domesticam* seu *oeconomicam* in suos subditos et publicam administrationem gerunt, qua plura externa munia vi officii explent." Cf. Rossi, De Paroecia, pp. 70-71.

[8] Cc. 83, 1043-1046, 1245.

[9] De Paroecia, p. 73.

[10] Cc. 90-96, and 87.

[11] Can. 1350.

which he exercises the care of souls be conferred upon him *"in titulum."* About the nature of a parish more detail shall be given in the second part of this chapter. The phrase conferred *"in titulum"* must be considered somewhat carefully for the definition of title plays a conspicuous part in prescription and possession.

What is a title? Augustine in his commentary quotes the difinition of Reiffenstuel:[12] *"Titulus est justa causa possidendi quod nostrum non est."*[13] That is, a title is a legitimate cause for possessing what otherwise does not belong to one. Does not this seem a very general definition of the term? There is another notion of the expression somewhat more specifically technical in relation to the canonical ideas of parish and benefice. It is the descriptive definition though historical given in Kahl's Lexicon:[14] *"Tituli primum erant certae sedes clerecis attributae, in quibus munus exercent. Postea . . . praedia iis ad victum cultumque assignata."* That is, titles were the places where clerics exercised their ministry and from which they derived their livelihood. Is this definition not a rather exact notion applicable to the parishes of today?[15] There is a sort of contract by which the priest in virtue of his office is bound to minister to the spiritual needs of the members of his flock for which ministration they in return support him. Is this not more accurate than the notion conveyed by Augustine, in explaining the above-quoted definition of Reiffenstuel in the sense that the pastor is the possessor of the parish. Both Blat and Cocchi incline to this same interpretation.[16] Granting that the pastor is the possessor in the sense of *administrator* of the parish, as regards the temporalities, his *administration* is very much

[12] This definition of Reiffenstuel is not intended for the purpose for which it is used by Augustine, but is given in connection with a discussion on ownership through *prescription*.

[13] Cf. Augustine, Commentary II, p. 510 (c); Reiffenstuel, II, 26, 127.

[14] Cf. Joannis Kahl alias Calvini, Lexicon Magnum Juris Caesarei simul, et Canonici, Genevae, MDCLXXXIII, word, *Tituli*.

[15] Rossi says that by *"in titulum"* is meant a special moral union between the parish and pastor by which a priest becomes the proper rector or pastor of a parish, so that he receives his title from it, and is denoted by it, v. g. the pastor of *St. Matthew's*. Cf. Rossi, De Paroecia, p. 73, footnote (36).

[16] Blat. II, p. 483, n. 499; & Cocchi, Lib. II, pars. I, sec. II, Tit. VIII, cap. IX, n. 333 b.

restricted. Though the Code calls the pastor the *administrator* of the parish, inasmuch as it is a benefice, and all of our parishes in this country are indisputably benefices,[17] yet when it explains his powers of administration, it takes the word in the rather wide sense of *"curator."* Care must be taken not to confound the canonical use of the word *administrate* in relation to pastors with the latitude of the same word in its civil law signification.[18] For today in the *administrator* according to modern civil law very extensive powers are invested. He may dispose of the property which he administers according to his own discretion as if it were his own. He needs no permission for particular acts and as long as he is in good faith he is accountable to no one for the disposition he makes of the intestate's estate.

When a pastor has received a true title to the parish by which it is *canonically* his, so that he can administer it in his own name, the actual disposition he is empowered to make is very limited indeed. The Code clearly states that the *"beneficiarius"* should administer *"ut beneficii curator,"* [19] and elsewhere the Bishop is warned that he must sedulously see to the administration of all the ecclesiastical goods in his territory, which are not exempt from his jurisdiction.[20] Furthermore, the Pastor in his administration is under the eye of the Vicar Forane who, in his deanery, should be watchful, *"ut beneficialia bona conserventur et administrentur."* [21] The value of this legislation can be duly estimated by those bishops who have had pastors to burden small and comparatively poor parishes with heavy debts. Comprehending this legislation, certainly no pastor can consider himself the owner or proprietor of the parish or the temporal goods of the parish. If any one at all, it must be said that the Bishop is the proprietor of the parishes of his dioceses,

---

[17] Golden, Parochial Benefices in the New Code, Cap. IX.

[18] Code of District of Columbia, Cap. 5, Administration, 32, Stat. L, pt. I, p. 528, repealing 31 Stat. L, pt. I, p. 1189. Act of Maryland of 1798, ch. 101, subch. 5, sec. 4; Comp. Stat. D. C., p. 12, sec. 42. This legislation implies, it would seem, that the administrator is accountable only for maladministration.

[19] Canon 1476 §1.

[20] Canon 1519 §1.

[21] Canon 1478.

especially if he holds them as a corporation sole.[22] The Bishop, however, does not possess them personally in the sense that at the time of his death they become the property of his heirs, but rather he possesses them for the church.

The bishop should appoint the Special Committees to help the Pastor properly to regulate the temporalities of his parish. The bishop does not allow a pastor to undertake any sort of work which would involve debt without first obtaining his permission in writing.[23]

The third chapter of the third Plenary Council of Baltimore entitled, *"De Muneribus Sacerdotum Praesertim Rectorum,"* speaks of the administration of ecclesiastical goods by the Pastor, as being made "sub episcopi directione." In number 279 of that chapter, it lays down a rule, that if a church is to be erected, or even a school or rectory, or if any alterations or enlarging, or tearing down is to be done, then the Pastor must obtain in writing the permission of the Ordinary before proceeding. This order is given expressly so that useless and impossible debts may be avoided. This number of the *"Acta et Decreta"* of the Baltimore Council, furnishes much food for thought for parish priest even of this day and age. Notice the sound warning that the Fathers of that meeting thought it necessary to issue: **"Igitur strictissime prohibemus, vetamus et interdicimus, ne quis rector, sacerdos, et pii loci curator, sive ecclesiae sive missionis sive episcopi nomine ecclesiam suam vel locum aere alieno gravare quocumque titulo vel colore audeat, *sine expressa et scriptis exarata licentia* ordinarii."** *A fortiori* then the placing of debts on church property or goods for the benefit of the Pastor himself is forbidden, as the last paragraph of this same chapter of the proceedings naturally inculcates.[24]

Before leaving the subject of title there is but a word to be added anent presumptive title, *"titulus putativus."* For example, it may happen that a parish was always thought to have

[22] Cf. Augustine, Canonical and Civil Status of Parishes, p. 109 ff.; S.C.C. July 29, 1911 (Ecclesiastical Review, 1911, vol. 45, p. 585); cf. canons 1409; 1489 §1, 1495 §2; 1499 §2, 99, 100 §2.

[23] Cf. Tit. XXVIII, cc. 1518-1529; 1182-1184. For borrowing what exceeds a certain amount, permission of the Holy See is required. Cf. cc. 1530-1533.

[24] Acta et decreta Conc. Baltimorensis, III. Baltimore, 1886. Care must be taken not to overestimate the ruling of the Council of Baltimore, especially inasmuch as it may have been corrected by the Code. Then, too, despite the title *"Acta et Decreta,"* the declaration of papal indults is confused at times with conciliar enactments.

been conferred on the "de *facto parochus*," but unfortunately no document to that effect can be found. At times the Pastor's right to such a parish may be questioned. This case in the past has been more frequent in reference to moral persons and to the Pastors of parishes under "*juspatronatus*" than to Pastors appointed directly by the Bishop. In such a case a parish may then be claimed by prescription, if the holder "*de facto*" was in good faith during all the time required for prescription. The present ecclesiastical legislation does not lay down any ruling to the contrary, as it does not mention anything whatsoever concerning the nature of the "*titulus*." [25] In Canon 1446, which speaks of benefices in general, we find a rule which may be applied to parishes. "*If a cleric who possesses a benefice shall have proved that he had the pacific possession for three full years in good faith, although by chance with an invalid title, provided it is not invalid from simony, he obtains the benefice from legitimate prescription.*[26]

The third characteristic of the Pastor is that in the discharge of his functions and duties, he is always subject to the Bishop of the diocese. It has been said that his power is ordinary in the sense that it is attached to the office, and defined by universal ecclesiastical law. This does not mean, however, to say that it is independent, for it is what some authors call "*vicaria*" or "*relative ordinaria*." [27] The power of a Pastor does not exclude that of the Bishop, since the latter possesses and can exercise ordinary jurisdiction in every part of the diocese of which he is the Pastor. It is true, as Bouix says, that in the strict sense of the word, comprising the offices of teacher, sanctifier, and judge or ruler, the title of Pastor belongs in an especial manner to the successors of the apostles who are the Bishops. This in no way detracts from the honor and office of the parish Priest. There is no reason why two or three should not exercise jurisdiction over the same people, provided their jurisdictions are "*inter se*" *dependent*,[28] for just as the Bishop is pastor of the whole diocese so the Pope is pastor of the entire world. In

[25] Cf. Can. 451 §1; cf. Rossi, De Paroecia, pp. 179-180.

[26] This is taken probably from Rule 36 of the Apostolic Chancery entitled "*De triennali possessione*," cf. Wernz, Jus Decretalum IV, n. 448.

[27] Cf. Wernz-Vidal Jus Canonium, II, n. 365, c. p.

[28] Cf. Scti. Thomae, Summa Theologia, Suppl. q. 8, 2, 5, ad. 3.

consequence of this principle, the Bishop could for grave reasons, delegate another priest to exercise parochial functions in a parish against the will of the Pastor, but this only in particular cases.[29] The power of a pastor though not independent cannot be restricted without a legitimate cause, nor so diminished as to lose its character.[30] His is an ordinary power granted by virtue of his office which the Bishop cannot take away arbitrarily nor reduce to an empty title. It is likewise undeniable, as the Code puts it, that this power must be depended upon and subject to that of the Bishop, and therefore the Pastor must exercise the care of souls under the Ordinary of the place. Thus it is none the less exercised *"vice et nomine alterius."* [31]

II. *The Religious Pastor*

This matter may be treated very briefly in this essay, as the topic of religious can furnish abundant material for a whole dissertation by itself. According to Canon 451, §1, the Pastor may be a moral person. In that case the moral person is merely what is called elsewhere in the Code the habitual pastor, for the moral person is directed to appoint, with the approval of the Bishop of the place, an individual physical person to be the actual pastor.[32] The moral person may be a community consisting of originally at least three persons or members, for example, a university in its primitive sense, a monastery or a chapter, in fine all such corporations. So also an institute, with a determined juridical nature and possessing rights granted for the

[29] Responsum S. C. C. in Aturensi, 14 Aug., 1862, citatum a Rossi, De Paroecia, p. 73.

[30] Cf. Bened. De Syn., lib. 5, cap. 4, n. 3; Bargilliat, Praelectiones, J. C., n. 839.

[31] Cf. Wernz-Vidal, Jus Canonicum, vol. II, footnote 1; n. 366. This is further supported by the very wording of Titles 7 and 8 of the Code. Tit. VII, De Suprema Potestate deque iis qui, ejusdem sunt ecclesiastico jure *participes*. Tit. VIII De Potestate episcopali deque iis qui de eadem *participant*. In cap. IX, under this title are treated *Parochi*. The pastor shares the power of the bishop, because his office is of ecclesiastical institution. The bishop's office is of divine institution and his power is ordinary. He does not participate in the Pope's power, as the pastor does in that of the bishop. Thus there are two offices in the Church to which are by divine institution attached ordinary jurisdiction, viz., the Pope's, over the whole Church and the Bishop's over the whole diocese.

[32] Cf. Canon 452, No. 2 and Carmignani, Il Piccolo Codice, Capo II.

end or purpose for which it was instituted comes under this heading. Therefore, hospitals or orphanages may be habitual pastors of a parish. In this wise, corporations and institutes represented by their procurators are called the habitual parish priests, to differentiate them from the actual pastor, who *"de facto"* and *"de jure"* exercises the care of souls. The following canon treats of the very union itself of the moral person with the parish, wherefore a few remarks concerning that subject will be made in passing as we quote that rule in its place. Suffice it to explain here that when a religious community has been given a parish, not all the priests of the community, if it be a clerical one, can be considered as having the actual care of souls, but only the actual pastor who in the Code is called the *"Vicarius perpetuus."* Otherwise confusion would result.[33] If the parish is entrusted to a particular religious, e. g., when there is a shortage of priests in a diocese, he is then called pastor.[34]

[33] Canon 456, §1 and 471.

[34] Cf. Faculties of Apostolic Delegates, n. 48, quoted by Vermeersch-Creusen, Epitome, Ed. of 1927, I, p. 527. The religious pastor, if a parish church is attached to a religious institute, should not be the same as the Superior of the house. Cf. Carmignani, II Piccolo Codice, Capo II, p. 7, footnote (2); also page 5, footnote (1).

CHAPTER XIV

The Parish

I. *Definition of a Parish*

A parish is by some considered as a portion of a diocese in which there is situated a church frequented by the inhabitants of that district. Formally considered a parish canonically is much more than is implied in this material point of view. It may be defined as a certain territory, circumscribed by fixed limits in which dwell faithful assigned to a certain priest, who exercises officially the care of souls over them in that place. Or again one might call it the gathering of the faithful living within a territory marked off by well defined limits over whom a proper priest is placed to exercise the care of souls. (*"Territorium cujuslibet dioecesis dividatur in distinctas partes territoriales; unicuique autem parti sua peculiaris ecclesia cum populo determinato est assignanda, suusque peculiaris rector, tamquam proprius ejusdem pastor, est praeficiendus pro necessaria animarum cura."*) Thus can be distinguished in this definition of a parish four essential elements: first, a distinct part of territory; second, a determined people; third, a parochial church, and fourth, the proper pastor.

II. *The Essential Notes of a Parish*

Whatever may be said about the historical origin of parishes, it must be maintained that for many centuries, the practice obtained in the Church for the sake of convenience and utility, to divide the faithful into territorial units. The obligation, however, of so doing was not imposed on the universal church before the Council of Trent. *"In iis civitatibus ac locis ubi nullae sunt parochiales (ecclesiae), quamprimum fieri curent (episcopi), non obstantibus quibuscumque privilegiis et consuetudinibus, etiam immemorabilibus. In iis (vero) . . . civitatibus ac locis, ubi parochiales Ecclesiae certos non habent fines, nec earum rectores proprium populum, quem regant. . . . mandat Sancta Synodus Episcopis . . . ut, distincto populo in certas propriasque Parochias, unicuique suum perpetuum peculiaremque Parochum assignent."* [1] This is the legislation that the Code itself has adopted in Canon 216. Aside from the implication of Canon 454, §3, the new law of the Code makes no specifications about parishes, as to their erection. In this respect they come under the ordinary rules for the erection of benefices.

The first of the four notes special to the parish as outlined in the definition given above is that it must be a distinct part of the diocese marked off by well defined limits. Now this is necessary in order that several priests might not be ministering to the same people as their pastors. Great confusion would result if more than one shepherd claimed the same parishioners as members of their flock.

Naturally the principle or source of division of the faithful is territorial. All Christians who live in the limits of a certain territory are considered to form a peculiar and separate flock or community distinct from the rest and consequently for convenience are constituted under a proper and peculiar pastor. For it is a commonly accepted fact that in human societies peoples and nations are divided one from another according to the proper and distinct territory. Therefore, divisions by which the mass of any people is cut into parts for the expediting of civil government are precisely territorial, as this is the most convenient. The same manner of acting holds good in the Church also, for as the number of Chistians is immense, they could not be taken care of adequately otherwise than by dividing them into territorial units. This is, however, not the only source of division for parishes as other vicissitudes and circumstances must come into play.

The next essential note of the parish is that there be a determined people over whom the *"proprius et peculiaris"* pastor rules. Here that is determined by the territory. It includes all the inhabitants baptized, non-Catholic as well as Catholic,[2] in the manner that has already been pointed out. It excepts

---

[1] Cf. Canon 216, §1, Wernz, Jus Decretalium, II, p. 2, tit. 29, §1.

[2] Cf. Canon 87.

only those communities or institutes which enjoy the privilege of exemption.

However, the new legislation has, in the matter of receiving the Sacraments from the *"proprius parochus,"* made some change. Formerly, for instance, the ruling of the Council of the Lateran (1215)[3] which attempted to render uniform the practice of the Church as regards the reception of Holy Communion, did not specify any place for the reception of the Paschal Communion, but the discipline of the time clearly pointed to the parish church. Very close bonds then united the faithful to the parish priest and church. It was the pastor who was the *"sacerdos proprius" of the Council; "a quo solo licite sacramenta suscipient."* It is not surprising then to find particular Councils commanding the faithful to go to their parish church and clergy for the Paschal Communion. By custom and the explicit or implicit approval of the Holy See, this became a general obligation.[4]

The present law has not maintained that obligation, or discipline. It favors the reception of Communion at Easter in one's own parish, and asks that it be recommended to the faithful, but does not impose it as an obligation. Those who make their Easter duty outside the parish church are only requested to notify their parish priest. This request has the form of a command, and imposes an obligation but not a grave one, as the matter does not call for it.[5] The Code further has regulated the obligation of contracting marriage before the *"proprius parochus,"* as is well known, together with administration of the other sacraments.[6]

The last essential note of the parish to be considered here, is the parish church, for the others have been treated already. This requires that for each parish there be its own proper church building, or place where the parishioners assemble as such to profess that they are members of one spiritual society. It is here that most of the sacraments and sacramentals are administered and where they are strongly exhorted to hear the word of God and finally it is whence they are borne to their last

---

[3] Cf. Caput 21, IV Conc. Lateranense, Apud. Den., p. 194.

[4] Cf. Ayrinhac, Legislation on the Sacraments, p. 178, n. 154.

[5] Cf. Canon 859; especially §3; Vermeersch-Creusen, n. 128; Blat., p. 194; Capello, n. 475; DeMeester, p. 271, n. 825.

[6] Cf. Canon 462, 467, and also Raia, De Parochis, p. 56, footnote 4; Bouix, De Parocho, C. III; cf. Canon 1094; Fanfani, p. 287, n. 307.

resting place. A parish is sometimes identified with this sacred building dedicated to divine worship, whereas, it is used chiefly for their public religious service. No church may be constructed without the express consent of the local Ordinary given in writing.[7] The Vicar General needs a special mandate for granting this consent.[8]

III. *The Parishes in the United States Are All Canonical*

The history of the Church in this country has been one of constant growth and approach to the condition of those countries which have been under the rule of common law for centuries. In the beginning French and Spanish settlements brought from their native countries very definite ideas about church discipline, but contrary to expectation these did not last. The parishes and benefices which they erected have all vanished. Shea, in his history of the Church, quotes the first Council of Baltimore as mentioning the only known benefice in the United States as in New Orleans,[9] and quotes the Synod of New Orleans of 1844 as stating that there were no benefices in that diocese.[10] The same author says that canonical parishes were erected in New Mexico in 1801.[11] Shea also speaks of the displeasure of certain parties in both Californias over the establishment of canonical parishes in 1841.[12] Putzer in his first edition of the Commentary on Apostolic Faculties (1886), tells us the Provincial Council of San Francisco hints that there are, in the province of San Francisco, canonical parishes ruled over by missionary priests not having the status of pastors.[13]

The Church had its greatest growth in the colonies settled by the people other than French or Spanish, and whatever of the common law practices the Spanish and the French had intro-

---

[7] Needless to say the Church should be in the confines of the parish. (Cf. c. 1164.) The building itself should not communicate with the house of a layman.

[8] Cf. Fanfani, De Jure Parochorum Titulus II, De Ecclesia Parochiali; cf. cc., 1162 §1, 1164 §1, 467 §2.

[9] Vol. III, p. 414.

[10] Vol. IV. p. 269.

[11] Vol. IV, p. 298.

[12] Vol. IV, p. 352.

[13] Putzer, Apostolic Faculties, Ed. of 1886, n. 130.

duced, were soon lost. The American Catholic Church started from very crude beginnings, and under such circumstances that it was impossible to conform to the laws governing parishes and the like. When the first bishop of Baltimore appointed priests, he sent them out with a sort of general care of the people in a more or less indefinite territory. Lack of organization, scarcity of priests, fluctuating population and lack of funds, were among the reasons which compelled him to do the best he could under circumstances, without adhering strictly to the ideal methods prescribed by the common law.

The second and third plenary councils of Baltimore (as has already been brought out in the historical part of this essay) gradually adapted as much of the common law of the Church to this country as was feasible, and in keeping with the regulations of the Congregation of the Propaganda, under which the United States was until 1908. After 1908 this country came under the common law of the Church, and with the promulgation of the Code, our parishes became *canonical* parishes and hence for their erection and status must follow the ruling of it.

Nor can refuge be taken from this course of the law that the parishes of the United States are not *canonical* parishes, due to the fact that some lack more or less the essential note of well defined limits. If there are not well defined limits, there are some sort of limits, customary or otherwise. If there were not, there would be no *"modus vivendi"* between neighboring pastors, no matter how great be the distance which separates them. Custom in these cases marks off the boundaries which a bishop has failed to define and prescription will make them sure. Abuses in this matter were condemned both by the Council of Trent and by the particular legislation of this country. Of course, certain and definite limits and boundaries of parishes should not be infringed upon ordinarily or at least not without some good reason.

That the parishes in this country are *canonical* is evident from a letter sent by the former Apostolic Delegate, the then Archbishop Bonzano of happy memory, to all the bishops of this country on November the tenth, 1922. In this letter he gives the reply he received from Cardinal Gasparri, the Cardinal, Prefect of the Commission for the Authentic Interpretation of the

Code of Canon Law, concerning the following *dubium:* (*Ia. pars*). Is it necessary that the Ordinary should issue a formal decree declaring explicitly that he erects a certain district into a parish; or (*IIa, pars*) is it sufficient that, having divided a certain territory into several districts, the respective limits of which are definitely indicated, he assigns to each district a rector to take charge of the people and the church thereunto pertaining, according to Canon 216 §1 and §3? In a second *dubium* he asked further if after the promulgation of the Code, a special decree on the part of the Ordinary was necessary to constitute as *canonical* parishes those which previous to the promulgation of the Code, had been established in the manner described in the first part of the *"dubium"* as quoted above. The answer to this was that no decree was necessary, and that such parishes, ipso facto, on the promulgation of the Code became *canonical* parishes. To the first *"dubium,"* under date of September 26, 1921, His Eminence Cardinal Gasparri answered, *"Negative ad primam partem,"* i. e., that a special decree of the Ordinary is not necessary for the erection of a parish; and *"Affirmative ad secundam partem,"* i. e., that it is sufficient, *"quoad hoc,"* for the erection of a parish, that the Ordinary define the territorial limits and assign a rector to the people and the church within said limits.[14]

His Eminence the President of the Commission added moreover that a parish is always an ecclesiastical benefice, according to Canon 1411, §5, whether it has the proper endowment (resources or revenue) as described in Canon 1410, or even, if lacking such endowment, it is erected according to the provisions of Canon 1415, §3.

In the words of the late Cardinal Bonzano, "It is evident that all the parishes of the United States having the three necessary qualifications, viz., 1, a resident pastor; 2, endowment (resources or revenue according to the provisions of Canons 1410 and 1415, §3); and 3, boundaries, are not only parishes in the canonical sense, but are *ecclesiastical benefices.* Hence pastors in the United States are real *canonical* pastors (*parochi*), having all the duties and obligations, etc." This official answer was in keeping with the Code as well as with the Declaration of the

[14] Apostolic Delegation, No. 3096-F. This letter is quoted in full by Augustine, "Canonical and Civil Status of Parishes," p. 63 ff.

S. C. Consistorialis of August 1, 1919, where the three conditions were expressly mentioned; a, resident pastor; b, endowment; c, boundaries, and the Ordinaries were told that they might erect subsidiary churches or chaplaincies, but only within the limits of *canonical* parishes.[15] Be it remarked that these subsidiary churches or chapels are always dependent upon the *canonical* parish.

IV. *The Parishes in the United States Are Benefices*

If our parishes are not *canonically* erected, they cannot be benefices. The two ideas are practically inseparable, and are considered so by the Code, which gives certain phases of legislation for them under the *title of parishes,* and other phases under *that of benefices.* It is not impossible to conceive a parish which is not a benefice, but it surely is impossible to conceive a benefice with the care of souls which is not at the same time a *canonical* parish.

It might seem strange that the Code contains no special paragraphs describing the formalities required for the valid and licit erection of parishes. With the exception of Canons 216 §1, 451, 454, and 455, it is apparently silent concerning this *conditio sine qua non.* However, there can be no doubt that the Code intends to have applied also to parishes the laws governing benefices. This is manifest from several canons which occur in *Book III, Title XXV, De Beneficiis,* where parishes are expressly mentioned.[16]

If it is granted that the parishes in this country are *canonical,* then consideration must be given to the question of benefices. Three things are necessary for a benefice: First, the sacred office; secondly, the right to the revenues of the endowment, and lastly the erection. That our parishes have the sacred office is beyond doubt or question. They have the second condition if to the sacred office is attached the right to receive the revenue from the certain and voluntary offerings of the faithful, or stole fees, or both. For these are the usual and possible sources of parish revenue here. It is well to note that it is not necessary that this revenue be sufficient for the support of the rectors, as there

[15] A. A. S., 1919, vol. XI, 364.

[16] Cf. cc. 1423, 1425-7.

is nothing in the definition [17] to that effect. Canon 1415 states that a benefice should not be erected unless with a sufficient endowment, but this does not imply that if the endowment is not suitable, the erection is invalid. There is no invalidating clause in Canon 1415. Besides, a suitable endowment will not always imply a sufficiency for the maintenance of the rector, as in the case of compatible benefices. The third condition shall be discussed after the second has been explained.

But have American pastors the second condition, namely, have they the right to the revenue coming from the parish benefice? Have they the right to certain and voluntary offerings of the faithful? The certain and voluntary offerings of the faithful in this country come in the form of pew rents, block collections, yearly dues, Christmas and Easter collections, and the like. Pastors here receive, not these certain and voluntary offerings, but stated salaries, and the salaries are considered as the amount of beneficial revenue necessary for their decent support, either with or without living expenses, according as to how the salary is regulated. Can one say then that pastors here receive the revenue of the parish or benefice? It seems that one can, and that the circumstances of the country permit the bishops to determine just how much revenue the pastor needs, in harmony with the long standing custom of determining the salary. Even if one must concede that the disposition of superfluous goods must be permitted beneficiaries without any interference from their bishop, is it not rather the present system must be changed, than that one must conclude that the parishes are not benefices? Once it is decided that the parishes here are canonical, then the conclusion that they are likewise benefices and come under the laws governing this sort of entity cannot be denied.

Canon 1415 appears to make an exception for parishes that have not sufficient revenue, but where can be found any regulations for parishes which are canonical, have the sufficient revenue, and still are not benefices? The Code, which is supposed to be the collection of all the universal laws governing the organization of the Church, does not legislate for such a parish. Can it be presumed that there is a lacuna in the Code? When one

---

[17] Canon 1410.

looks for the division, union, erection and the like, of parishes, one finds it under the title of benefices.

It should be recalled that there is a change in the very definition of benefices—the omission of the perpetual right to receive revenue; and a change in the constitution of the endowment of a benefice, so as to include, for example, stole fees. A new distinction is made with regard to pastors, namely, their division into removable and irremovable species. It would be interesting to know why these changes were made if not for the very purpose of including such places as the United States under the common law with regard to both parishes and benefices, and making it easier to accomplish this end by accommodating the law to the circumstances of the places. The whole history of the Church in this country has been one of gradual approach to the common law of the Church, and now it appears that the universal law is coming down to our level, so to speak, to meet the condition. What grounds, therefore, has anybody to try to evade the issue when it is put so clearly? It seems that the burden of the proof is on one who objects to the conclusion that the parishes of this country are benefices.

The third condition of a benefice is erection. Ecclesiastical authority must intervene in the erection of benefices. The Sovereign Pontiff, by virtue of his plenitude of power, can erect benefices of any sort, in any part of the world, and to him is reserved the erection of certain forms of benefices. And as he is above all canon law, he is not bound by its prescriptions except in so far as they are declarations of divine law.

For other benefices below the episcopacy and that of the Cathedral Chapter, the authority of the Ordinary is sufficient, whether the Ordinary be a bishop or a vicar or prefect apostolic having quasi-episcopal authority.[18] This is drawn from the constant and long standing discipline of the Church. For in former times, by authority of the bishop, clergy were deputed to perform certain sacred functions, and on account of them they receive the revenue necessary for their support. During the course of time, after the clergy ceased to live a common life, the bishops themselves distributed the immovable goods of the church to each member of the clergy serving the churches,

[18] A prefect apostolic may lack the episcopal character.

so that each one received in perpetuity a certain portion of the ecclesiastical goods by reason of his office.

Having established the fact of the endowment sufficient for the decent support of the clergy of the benefice, it is the duty of the bishop, before he erects the benefice, to invite and hear the opinions of all those concerned, namely, the pastors of neighboring parishes, parishioners and others who may have to contribute or who may suffer detriment. However the omission of this formality does not invalidate the erection of a parish.[19] The erection is then made by a legitimate document or public writing in which is defined the place, the revenue, rights and duties of the beneficiaries, and this is placed in the archives so as to be ficiaries, and this document is placed in the archives so as to be available in case of necessity, to determine right in the case of any conflict which may arise. Just as the calling of the interested parties is not necessary for validity, so also the drawing up in a public document of the fact of erection is not for validity, and its omission will not affect the canonical status of the parish or benefice. Be it always remembered that the parishes in the United States, whether they be removable or irremovable, are all benefices.

V. *National and Personal Parishes*

Though the territorial limits seem to be the essential mark by which parishes are numerically distinct, this is not an exclusive characteristic without which parishes cannot be canonically erected. There are some whose distinction is not territorial but *national, racial,* or *personal,* or *according to rite.* There may exist side by side in the same territory Catholics who belong to different *rites.* Then the Church is careful as far as

---

[19] Cf. Rossi: De Paroecia, pp. 28 seqq., n. 34, Formalities "Locorum Ordinarii . . . divisiones, dismembrationes beneficiorum ne faciant nisi . . . auditis . . . iis, si qui sint, quorum intersit, praesertim rectoribus ecclesiarum (Can. 1428, §1). Sed *"invitis* quoque earum *rectoribus et sine populi consensu"* postquam auditi sunt, Ordinarius ad paroecias dismembrandas aut dividandas procedere pleno jure potest (cf. Can. 1427, §1). Etiam in locis missionum audiendus est rector ecclesiae dismembrandae quia "ubi lex non distinguit, nec nos distinguere debemus" et quia in Constitutione "Romanos Pontifices," Leo XIII, S. M. apertis verbis statuit ut "sententia quoque rectoris exquiratur" aut "praefectus ordinis audiatur" si missio religiosis administranda demandata sit.

possible to provide that all the members of one *rite,* congregate in their own proper church and be cared for by their own proper pastor. This is done that they may more easily communicate in that rite which they understand and with which they are familiar. It so happens that to a great extent the faithful of the Oriental or other *rites* live in mixed surroundings, for which cause the Church has so organized them, that each rite has its own patriarch, as head of the whole rite, or at least its own archbishops, bishops and pastors. Likewise in the Orient live not a few Latins who, of course, are not subject to the Oriental prelates, but have their own religious superiors, such as the Patriarch of Jerusalem and Apostolic Delegates in other regions, etc. If in any diocese or country, where Orientals are to be found in very large number, there is *not* a *proper* bishop for them, the Ordinary of the place should provide for them a Vicar General, together with pastors and churches.

Another basis of the division into parishes is the circumstance of language. If in a diocese there dwell a considerable proportion of families who do not speak the language of the place, parishes should be established for them, of which the pastor is either of their own nationality or at least speaks their language fluently. Even these parishes along with those spoken of above are to some extent territorial, though that fact does not pertain to the essence in the same way as for other parishes. Generally speaking, the territory alloted to them embraces that of several of the native parishes, so that it would seem that two pastors have jurisdiction over the same ground. However, this fact does not seem to militate against the *canonical* status of such parishes as described in Canon 216 §4.[20] Somewhat different, strange to say, is the condition of the rural national parishes, which, owing to the fact that they often extend over an indefinite territory, seem to lack one of the essential features of a canonical parish. But like the question referred to earlier in this chapter even these parishes have customary boundaries.

Undeniably there is a certain danger to such parishes, for the people are politically one with the people who speak the vernacular of the country. In the Code, Canon 216, §4, forbids

---

[20] Cf. Rossi, De Paroecia, p. 21, §30, c. where he implies that there should be 10 families or homes for the starting of a new parish. Cf., also Cap. Unio, 3, caus., 10, q. 3.

the erection of new parishes of this kind without an indult [21] from the Holy See. This fact seems to indicate that the Church is restricting their multiplication. Moreover, the rules of the Chancery require that bishops of dioceses in which there is a mixture of tongues spoken both learn and speak the languages of the people. Is it not after all much easier to have *national* parishes in a diocese of various *nationalities,* than to have a distinct and separate diocese with an individual bishop for each of these *nationalities?* Another form of national parish is that found particularly in the city of Rome. In that city there are a number of people who though of different *nations* all speak the language of the place, but in reality they are only colonists. These people too have been allowed to have their own national churches, which cannot be erected without a *"beneplacitum apostolicum."*

According to some there is a solid doubt about our national parishes being benefices, because (as they claim) "they are actually and almost necessarily more or less subsidiary and fluctuating." [22] To say that they are subsidiary is not absolutely true, because their standing has been recognized by the Code as independent from the parish within the limits of which they are erected.[23] It is true that the Code prohibits the erection of new parishes of this kind, but it explicitly permits the existing national parishes to keep their identity, and therefore, their independence from the territorial parish. And are they necessarily fluctuating? Have not such parishes been established for years and with no prospect of dropping out of existence? It is not necessary that a parish be guaranteed to last forever before it may be erected. Otherwise what is the purpose of the law on suppression of benefices? The only requisite in this regard is that it be permanently established regardless of whether or not it afterwards becomes unnecessary. Many of the present territorial parishes will most likely lose most or all of their present parishioners when economic conditions in this district change. We think, then, that even the *national* parishes have

---

[21] Cf. A. A. S., vol. XVI (1924), p. 113. Even in countries such as Canada, where there are several official languages, permission of the Holy See is required to erect national parishes.

[22] Augustine, op. cit., vol. VI, p. 495.

[23] Canon 216, 4.

equally as much right to the name "*canonical*" parish and benefice as the territorial parish, provided the other conditions are present. According to the decree of the Sacred Congregation of the Consistory,[24] there is mentioned as subsidiary churches, those churches which, on account of the small number of people or of the fluctuating population, or absolute lack of suitable means of support cannot be erected into parishes. The fluctuating population here mentioned cannot be applied to national parishes, because members of *national* parishes are no more of a fluctuating nature in this country than the members of the territorial parish. The only difference is one of language and their residence is as permanently fixed as that of those who at present speak the vernacular tongue.

Lastly, it might be well in passing to refer here to another category of parishes of rather infrequent occurrence, namely, *family or personal* parishes. A *family* parish might be constituted for a Royal House or an Ambassador and his retinue. A *personal* parish might be established for soldiers or a colony of exiles. It is well known that military chaplains receive special faculities for their work.[25] As to such parishes if they already exist, they cannot be changed without consulting the Holy See, and a new one cannot be erected without an indult from the Holy See. When there is a Royal Parish, its pastor usually enjoys special privileges, and his jurisdiction commonly extends to several different places.

No. 1 of paragraph 2 of this Canon 451 says that *quasi-pastors* who rule *quasi-parishes* are equivalent to pastors with all their rights and obligations. The territorial divisions of the Vicariates and Prefectures Apostolic are divided into parts known as quasi-parishes.[26] These still follow the Instructions of the Propaganda.[27]

[24] 1 August, 1919, A. A. S. XI.

[25] As to military chaplains, some canonists used to consider them all as personal pastors, but the Code in Canon 451, §3, contains no such formal provision; it only refers to the special arrangement made by the Holy See in the different countries and which it leaves unchanged. In this country we have a military bishop (Episcopus castrensis) or major chaplain with authority over minor chaplains, who obtain their powers from him.

[26] Cf. Canon 216.

[27] Cf. July 25, 1920, A. A. S., XII, p. 331, for missionary countries with bishops; cf. S. C. Prop. Fide, Dec. 9, 1920; n. 1, n. 2, n. 3, A. A. S. XIII, 17.

1. It is the mind of the sacred canons that the territory of Vicariates and Prefectures Apostolic be divided into distinct parts, each of which should have a determined people, with a proper church, and a peculiar pastor.[28] Wherefore Vicars and Prefects Apostolic should strive to organize thus the Missions entrusted to them, and where they judge it possible, they should not omit to introduce this arrangement.

2. This division is not to be urged hastily or inconsiderately, especially if it be seen that those things which are necessary, will be wanting.[29] Vicars and Prefects Apostolic, in erecting *quasi-parishes,* should keep before their eyes the good of souls, and the means whereby Catholicism can spread in their regions. Hence the matter should be examined seriously, and the counsel heard according to Canon 302, or at least the opinion of three of the principal Missionaries, assembled, or in the manner described in Canon 303.

3. It is not necessary nor should it be urged that one wait until the time be fully ripe for the dividing of the entire territory of Vicariates or Prefectures into *quasi-parishes;* for one can proceed gradually and partially yet usefully, so that one part may be divided into *quasi-parishes* before the opportune time to divide the rest has arrived.

4. The erection of quasi-parishes should be by the decree of the Ordinary in which the territorial limits are to be clearly defined. But where this practice cannot obtain, it suffices that there be a declaration, which Christian communities belong to the particular *quasi-parishes.* In the decree, it should be especially stated, what is the principal Church of the *quasi-parish,* and where the *quasi-pastor* resides.

5. Two copies of the decree should be made, one for the Archives of the Vicariate or Prefecture Apostolic, the other to be kept in the acts of the newly erected *quasi-parish.*

6. Once the *quasi-parish* has been constituted, *ipso facto,* arise all the rights and obligations of the *quasi-pastor,* which have been sanctioned by the Code of Canon Laws (especially, Canons 451, §2, 1; 454, §4; 456; 459; 461; 1356; 306; 462; etc.).

7. For the celebration of Matrimony, in duly erected *quasi-*

[28] Can. 216, §2.

[29] Can. 1415, §3.

parishes, Canons 1095 and 1096 must be followed; but in places where they have not been so constituted, the Missionaries are to be considered the *"cooperatores"* of the Vicar or Prefect Apostolic, and hence with the general permission granted by the Ordinary, they, validly and licitly, assist at marriages.

8. Likewise it follows from the erection of a *quasi-parish,* that all chapels, or oratories, within the limits of the territory of the *quasi-parish,* are to be considered as subsidiary and remain in their dependence until they are constituted as *quasi-parishes* or are given exemption from the care of the *quasi-pastor,* according to Canon 464.

9. After the division of the territory into *quasi-parishes* has been enacted, it will be most advisable that also the Vicariate or the Prefecture be portioned into districts comprising several *quasi-parishes,* as has already been done in some Vicariates, so that *Vicariatus foranei* may be foreshadowed, and more apt provision be made for the ruling and administration of the Mission.[30]

To pastors the present law likewise assimilates *parochial vicars* who have full charge of a parish: Such is the case of *vicars parochial* proper or *administrators,*[31] the *vicarii oeconomi,*[32] and sometimes of the *vicarii substituti* and *adjutores.*[33] Concerning military chaplains whether major or minor, the peculiar or special prescriptions of the Holy See for them must be adhered to.

VI. *Religious Parishes*

Canon 452

§1. Sine Apostolicae Sedis indulto paroecia nequit personae morali pleno iure uniri, ita nempe ut ipsamet persona moralis sit parochus, ad nornam Can. 1423, §2.

§2. Persona moralis, cui paroecia sit pleno iure unita, habitualem tantum curam animarum retinere potest, servato, quod ad actualem spectat, praescripto Can. 471.

---

[30] Canon 217, 445 et seqq.
[31] Cf. Canon 471.
[32] Cf. Canon 472.
[33] Cf. Canons 474, 475.

In general it may be said that without an Apostolic indult no parish can be united *"pleno jure"* to a moral person in such a way that the moral (i. e., juridical person) person would be the pastor. In this matter canonists distinguish a threefold mode of union; the first is *"plenissimo jure,"* which amounts practically to *"abbatia nullius"* or a territory juridically separated from the rest of the diocese, for example Belmont Abbey, North Carolina; the second is *"Pleno jure,"* i. e., when a parish is united to the moral body both for the possession and administration, in matters spiritual and temporal; the third is *"Semipleno Jure,"* by which a community or institute becomes the administrator of a parish in matters temporal,[34] but not in matters both spiritual and temporal at the same time. In the first and second cases, the parishes are truthfully called religious parishes, but in the third case they are in reality still secular parishes with a secular pastor.[35]

In order to erect a religious parish, an agreement must be made by both the Bishop and the religious community, then permission must be obtained from Rome. The Bishop will send his application to the Sacred Congregation of the Council while the religious community must address its application to the Sacred Congregation for Religious. If the two, i. e., Bishop and religious community are in agreement, the Holy See usually grants its *"Beneplacitum."* These same formalities must be observed if a secular parish is to be given to a religious order or institute. Whenever a Bishop proposes to erect such a parish, or to change a secular parish in such a manner, he should consult his diocesan consultors and those interested.[36] When a religious parish is divided by the Ordinary, who is the administrator of the whole diocese and consequently of every parish in it, the new parish, though formed from a religious parish, is

[34] Cf. Augustine, vol. II, Canon 453. Cf. Pistocchi, De Re Beneficiali, p. 101 seqq., p. 201 seqq.

[35] There can also be the case of a secular parish with a religious pastor. At times, owing to a dearth of secular priests, this becomes necessary. But then the parish is a secular parish still, the religious pastor is only temporary. The Apostolic Delegate has faculties to allow a bishop to make this arrangement. These faculties are referred to in a later footnote. Cf. Vermeersch-Creusen, I, p. 523.

[36] Cf. cc. 1425 to 1428.

a secular parish,[37] since a new religious parish cannot be erected without the permission of the Holy See. The consideration of the union called "*Semi-pleno Jure*" need not cause us much delay here, as it does not specifically come under this canon.[38] In all cases of religious parishes, the church building belongs to the diocese and the people of the parish, not to the religious community, so that if they give up the parish, they cannot exact remuneration for the building. The exception is the monastery, or abbey church, which is not parochial, but is frequented by a large number of people. Though the Holy See reserves to itself the establishment and division of religious parishes—even when such a parish is divided, the new parish is secular unless specified otherwise by the Holy See itself. As for the Ordinary's power to divide religious parishes, he can divide all except those belonging to exempt religious orders, whose boundaries have been explicitly and specifically designated in the "*beneplacitum apostolicum.*" For dividing these, the Ordinary needs the indult. Thus Canon 1427 must be interpreted in the light of 1422; for the Ordinary has no power over exempt religious. Canon 1422 is a general rule for all benefices, while Canon 1427 is to be taken as an exception for parochial benefices. When the Ordinary divides a religious parish the new parish is a secular parish,[39] unless he has obtained permission of the Holy See to make it a religious parish. Consequently the appointee should be a secular priest. Paragraph 2 of this Canon 452 has been treated sufficiently in the preceding chapter.

---

[37] For the dividing of religious parishes, according to Canon 1422 and 27. Cf. Golden, Parochial Benefices, p. 33, ff.

[38] Cf. c. 216; Chelodi, p. 368, c.; cf. Carmignani, II Piccolo Codice.

[39] Cf. Canon 1425, §5, "*divisa paroecia quae ad aliquam religionem jure spectat, vicaria perpetua aut paroecia noviter erecta non est religiosa.*"

CHAPTER XV

Qualifications of Pastors

Canon 453

§1. Ut quis in parochum valide assumatur, debet esse in sacro presbyteratus ordine constitutus.

§2. Sit insuper bonis moribus, doctrina, animarum zelo, prudentia, ceterisque virtutibus ac qualitatibus praeditus, quae ad vacantem paroeciam cum laude gubernandam jure tum communi tum particulari requiruntur.

I. Birth, Age, Orders

Looking back over the history of this question as contained in the first part of this dissertation, one cannot but be struck by the great advantage of this present ruling over that of the past. In an orderly consideration of the qualifications of the candidate for the parochial office, naturally one must begin at the beginning; in other words, is there any special requirement as to the birth of the appointee? Indirectly, at least "*legitima nativitas*" is demanded since no one can licitly be raised to sacred orders with this irregularity.[1] In the Code "*illegitimitas*" is included in the enumeration of irregularities "*ex defectu.*"

The next in order comes the age of the candidate. Although in the provision of ecclesiastical benefices, only that age is required which of itself is necessary that the appointee may fulfill the duties of the office in a becoming manner, yet generally the sacred canons prescribe a definite number of years and usually also at least indirectly what sacred orders must previously have been received. Thus the legitimate age of bishops is prescribed in Canon 331, §2; of the Vicar General Canon 367, §1; of the Vicar Capitular or administrator of a diocese

[1] Cf. Canon 968, §1, et Canon 984, §1.

"Sede Vacante," Canon 431, §1; the Canon Penitentiary 399, §1. Even in the old law the age of 25 years was demanded in the holder of a parochial benefice under the pain of nullity. The old legislation has been indirectly retained in the new. Inasmuch as generally speaking, the age of 24 completed, is demanded in all those about to be raised to the holy priesthood, by implication when the new law makes the requirement of the priesthood as an essential to the parochial office it demands also the age of 24 years completed.[2] But what of the case of one who is ordained to the holy priesthood with a dispensation from the impediment of age, before he has completed his 24th year? Can he be validly appointed to the position of parish priest? In the former legislation not the Bishop but the Holy See itself dispensed from the age required for the parochial office, which dispensation, at times, was granted. Be it remembered that the previous legislation required that the appointee be in his 25th year, i. e., that he should have completed his 24th birthday. Today the age is not explicitly mentioned at all, so that if one had been ordained to the holy priesthood with the dispensation from the requisite age, he could be appointed as pastor notwithstanding the fact that he had not yet completed his 24th year. This most likely is not an uncommon occurrence in many of the dioceses of this country.

After the consideration of the age in the candidate, sacredotal ordination is the next necessary qualification, and this is required under pain of nullity. As a general rule, the ecclesiastical benefices are reserved to clerics. *"Soli clerici possunt potestatem sive ordinis sive jurisdictionis ecclesiasticae et beneficia ac pensiones ecclesiasticas obtinere."* [3] Consequently the holder of such an office must be at least a tonsured cleric. Furthermore, the holder of a benefice to which the care of souls is attached should be a priest.[4] Evidently, else he could not exercise the functions of his office, e. g., he could not hear confessions; *"minister hujus sacramenti (poenitentiae) est solus sacerdos.*[5] This indicates a change from the earlier law, for by the usage

[2] Cf. Canon 975 ". . . presbyteratus (ne conferatur) ante vigesimum quartum (annum) completum."

[3] Cf. Canon 118.

[4] Cf. Canon 154; C. 15, de electione et electi potestate, I, 6, in VI.

[5] Cf. Canon 871.

and laws of the past a candidate could receive a parish *"in titulum"* whether he had already received the priesthood, or if having been only tonsured, he were so circumstanced as to be able to receive ordination to the priesthood within the space of one year. That this was at times the case, we can conclude with certainty from the fact that those who did not receive sacerdotal ordination within a year from the time of their peacefully taking possession of the parish, were to be deprived of it.[6] Another regulation was that if any one dared to accept a parish without the full intention of being advanced to the sacred order of the priesthood at the stated time, but merely from the motive of enjoying the benefits for a year, he had to renounce it, unless his intention had changed in that time and he received sacerdotal ordination. Otherwise, the income he had received was to be paid back. Such a condition of affairs was clearly recognized as dangerous and has been gradually avoided until the present legislation has developed from the experience of the past.[7]

The requirement of the priesthood concerns the validity of the appointment. The other qualifications to which attention is now to be paid refer rather to the liceity.[8] There is no doubt that in the pastor more than in the simple priest, knowledge and learning are to be desired; especially that knowledge which is conducive to a proper and fruitful administration of the sacraments, particularly the sacrament of penance. He should be able also to preach effectively the *"Word of God"* and should be generally well equipped for the care of the souls entrusted to him. In the seminary, of necessity, he has completed the course of studies prescribed by the Church and has been trained in ecclesiastical discipline.[9] But this training alone does not strictly suffice, for he should have experience of the ministry, otherwise he could give no proof of his ability. Canon 453, §2, inculcates that he should have all that is demanded both by common and particular law in the way of intellectual requirements and moral virtues. This has been very well paraphrased by Bargilliat,

[6] Cf. c. 14, VI, I, 6; Trid., Sess. 7, c. 3.

[7] Caput 7, §2, X De Elect., 6; cf. Rossi, De Paroecia, p. 77; footnote (44), (45), (46), (47).

[8] C. 7, X, de electione et electi potestate I, 6; c. 14, X, de officio judicis ordinarii, I, 31; Conc. Trid. Sess. XXI, de ref., c. 6.

[9] Cf. cc. 976, 993, §2.

"Praeter illas quae jure communi in promovendis requiruntur, exigi quandoque possunt et aliae qualitates ex privilegio, statuto, vel lege fundationis beneficii. . . "[10] Here, too, mention may be made of the second rule of the Chancery, which stipulates that the candidate for the office of pastor should be conversant in the vernacular of the parishioners and be able both to speak and write it fluently.

In conclusion the other requirement may be summed up as follows: Integrity and honesty, a reputation above suspicion, tact in dealing with the laity, prudence and discretion. *"Ministeria quae curam animarum habent adnexam nullus omnino suscipiat . . . nisi scientia et moribus commendatus existat."*[11] The pastor ought then to be a man of good habits, remembering always that his dignity is akin to that of the angels, and that in discharging the office of the good pastor he ought to express in his own life first, the piety and devotion which he wishes to inculcate in others. He ought to be the *"forma gregis ex animo."* When the canon uses the word *"doctrina,"* it has reference to the *office of the pastor* as teacher of the *"Word of God,"* which is impossible if he is not well versed in the sacred sciences.[12] These sciences include Theology, both Dogmatic and Moral, Sacred Scripture, Church History, Philosophy, and Canon Law.

But above all else there is needed in the encumbent of this office a true zeal for souls. The pastor, as it were, receives a spiritual paternity which requires in the words of St. Paul that "he beget Christ in the souls of men." In the careful discharge of his office he should strive always to do the right thing at the right time. He must be patient and painstaking, as well as charitable in speech and act. Finally, he ought to be adorned with all those virtues that will enable him laudably to fulfill the place of a Shepherd of the Flock. Since, for reasons of temperament, of culture, and of custom, one pastor differs from another, all are not suited for the same parish, nor are all suited for every parish.

Pope St. Gregory the Great says that the care of souls is the greatest of all arts. In words which he borrows from St. Gre-

---

[10] Cf. Praelectiones Juris Canonici, n. 209, seq.

[11] Cf. Constit., *"Cum in cunctis"* 7, De elect.

[12] Cf. Conc. Trid., Sess., 24, c. 18, De Ref. "Inter peccata distinguere, evangelium declarare, et sacramenta rite administrare."

gory Nazianzen, and which a thousand writers after him have placed at the head of their pastoral treatises, he expresses his profound conviction that to rule and guide souls a man must be an expert. Anyone who would take up such a task without the requisite skill and training would be inexcusably rash. He must first of all be a holy man. To be a physician of souls he must have at least learned the laws of the spiritual life. If a man teaches one thing and practices another, he is no pastor. He must be dead to his passions, insensible to pleasure, firm in adversity, and absolutely spiritual in all his views. St. Gregory begins the second book of the "*Regula pastoralis*"[13] with these words, "The pastor must excel his flock in conduct as much as the life of the shepherd ought to be above that of his sheep." This is St. Gregory's summary of a pastor's qualifications: 1. He must be pure in thought. 2. Excellent in behavior. 3. Discreet in silence and useful in speech. 4. Preeminently a man of contemplation. 5. Fraternizing with the good unaffectedly, while setting himself with just zeal against the offenses of the wicked. 6. Neither abandoning the interior for the exterior nor neglecting the exterior for the interior. The author of that excellent book, "Jesus Living in the Priest,"[14] says in describing the zeal that should be characteristic of every parish priest. "Zeal is the outgrowth of faith, the expression of sacrifice, the warmth of devotion." St. Ambrose says, "*Hic est zelus Dei; hic est fidei vapor, devotionis fervor.*" A zealous priest is one who ardently desires that God be known, loved and glorified, and that all men be saved. He is one who is ready to make every sacrifice and endure all things to extend the kingdom of God on earth and fill up the number of the elect. This was the habitual disposition of St. Paul, who in writing to the faithful of Corinth says, "I will most gladly spend and be spent for your souls."[15]

Hence it goes without saying almost that those whose lives are unworthy should be excluded from this office. In this class it is evident are to be counted criminals, infamous, excommunicated, suspended, interdicted, etc. No further comment need be made on men of these classes.

---

[13] Cf. Hedley, Lex Levitarum, London, 1906.

[14] Millet-Byrne, Jesus Living in the Priest, New York, 1901.

[15] Cf. II, Cor. XII, 15.

CHAPTER XVI

The Stability of the Pastor

Canon 454

§1. Qui paroeciae administrandae praeficiuntur qua proprii ejusdem rectores, stabiles in ea esse debent; quod tamen non impedit quominus omnes ab ea removeri queant ad normam juris.

§2. At non òmnes parochi eandem obtinent stabilitatem; qui majore gaudent, inamovibiles; qui minore, amovibiles appellari solent.

§3. Paroeciae inamovibiles nequeunt amovibiles reddi sine placito Apostolico; amovibiles possunt ab episcopo, non autem a Vicario Capitulari, de Capituli cathedralis consilio, inamovibiles declarari; novae quae erigantur, sint inamovibiles, nisi episcopus, prudenti suo arbitrio, attentis peculiaribus locorum ac personarum adjunctis, audito Capitulo, amovibilitatem magis expedire decreverit.

§4. Quasi paroeciae sunt omnes amovibiles.

§5. Parochi autem, ad religiosam familiam pertinentes, sunt semper, ratione personae, amovibiles ad nutum tam loci Ordinarii, monito Superiore, quam Superioris, monito Ordinario, aequo jure, non requisito alterius consensu; nec alter alteri causam judicii sui aperire multoque minus probare tenetur, salvo recursu in devolutivo ad Apostolicam Sedem.

I. *Stability Before the Code Outlined*

A proper explanation of this subject requires that by way of repetition a few introductory remarks be made first on the nature of benefices, together with a short historical outline of the development of the stability of the pastoral office. It is only then that one can adequately offer an exposition of the present legislation. In the preceding historical discussion, very little was said on the question of stability. The history of benefices brought into existence a new element in Church law, and this element was irremovability or perpetuity. The *"dos"* or source of revenue and the right to receive it were joined *"in perpetuum"* to the office, and this brought about a subjective perpetuity also, that is the incumbent of the office was permanently established in it for life, unless he resigned, was legitimately transferred, or was deprived according to the formalities of law. It is true that canonists make a distinction between temporary and perpetual benefices. *"Beneficia manualia et perpetua,"* but the *"beneficia curata"* or parochial benefices which have the care of souls attached to them, always belong to the latter class. In fact it seems to be the general opinion of canonists that *"beneficia manualia"* are only analogically called benefices, for since they are revocable at the will of the granter, they lack the essential element of stability required for an ecclesiastical benefice properly so called. This will suffice for the present, as this paper is not treating *"ex professo"* of benefices, but only of the appointment to *parochial benefices* or *canonical parishes.*

II. *History of the Stability of Pastors*

It has always been the mind of the Church that every pastor should be irremovable. Especially since the time of the Decretals it has manifested this desire repeatedly. The Council of Trent confirmed the legislation preceding it on this point when it said: *"unicuique (populo) suum perpetuum peculiaremque parochum assignent,"* [1] and the decree *"Maxima Cura"* repeated the same teaching by saying: *"praescriptum generatim fuit ut stabiles in suo officio permanerent."* [2]

The same decree gives us the fundamental reason for this teaching *"ut rectores quae paroeciae utilia aut necessaria esse indicarent alacriore possent animo suscipere, soluti metu ne ab ordinario amoverentur pro lubitu."* [3] Yet the stability was not

[1] Conc. Tridt. Sess., XXIV, de ref., c. 13.

[2] S. C. Conc., decr. *"Maxima Cura,"* August 28, 1910, proem., A. A. S., II, 636.

[3] Cf. Boudinhon, Inamovibilite, des Desservants, 35; Vacandard-Mangenot, Dict. de Theol. Cath. Art., Cure. Col. 2439, n. 77.

to be so essential to the parochial office as to exclude all possibility of removal therefrom. The above mentioned decree taught this very plainly; *"Nihilominus, quia stabilitas haec in salutem est inducta fidelium, idcirco sapienti cautum est, ut eadem non sic urgeatur, ut in pernicem potius ipsorum cedat."* This is but just, and in no way violates the rights of pastors, for whenever a pastor either through culpable faults or inculpable defects becomes incapable of attaining the end for which his office is instituted, namely, the welfare of souls, and instead becomes a hindrance to the same, the privilege of stability ceases in his regard and he can and must be removed.[4]

No trace of irremovability can be found as to the pastor, in church law before the origin of benefices properly so called.[5] Hence the opinion of Thomassinus that beneficiaries possessed this privilege in the first five centuries can be disputed. What he proves by the quotations he makes is rather that bishops could not depose or degrade and excommunicate clerics at will. Even when parishes began to be established in the fourth century, and priests began to acquire a certain degree of stability in them, in that they lived in the parish and were not merely sent to them as occasion required, they still remained removable *"ad nutum"* for any reason that the bishop deemed as sufficient.[6]

The Church did desire stability in those early centuries, but this stability applied more to the union of the cleric with the Church into which he had been, as it were, incardinated by ordination, than to any office to which he might have been promoted by the bishop.[7] This can be seen from some of the councils of the time.[8]

---

[4] Villien, Le Decret, *"Maxima Cura"* et le Deplacemant des Cures, 4; Greco, La Rimozione Amm. dei Parrochi, 16, sect. 7; Sebastianelli, apud Analect. Ecc. IV, 43.

[5] Stability or irremovability is that privilege by reason of which no one can be dispossessed of the office which he has received in title, except for reasons specified in law and through the observance of the formalities demanded by law.

[6] Nardi, Dei Parrochi, II, 481; Aichner, Comp. Juris Eccles., 423; Greco, La Rimoz, dei Parrochi, 15.

[7] Cf. Claeys-Bouuaert, o. c. 287; Ayrinhac, Constit. of the Church, p. 309, n. 252.

[8] Conc. Chalced, 451, Can. 6, Mansi, VII, 394; c. I. D., 70; Conc. Arlatense, I, 314; cc. 2 and 21, Mansi, II, 471, 473. Cf. Devoti, Institut. Canon, tom. I, tit. IV, sec. 2, 9; Claeys-Bouuaert, 287; Villien, 5; A. S. S., III, 507.

With the origin of benefices in the sixth century, however, the privilege of irremovability also began to be recognized. But it was not until the ninth century that various councils ordered that a certain amount of Church property be annexed to each parish, the revenues of which were to furnish sufficient means of support for the cleric. The doctrine of perpetual union of the cleric, through incardination, with the Church for which he had been ordained, was now transferred to the union with the benefice, so that, as the absolute ordinations had been forbidden before, so now ordinations *"sine titulo beneficii,"* were forbidden and declared invalid.[9]

The legislation of the Church even at this time recognized the privilege of irremovability of pastors not only because of the benefice attached to the office, but as pertaining to the nature of the office as such, independent of the benefice connected with it.[10]

The Council of Trent commanded not only the division of the people into parishes, but also, *"Unicuique suum perpetuum peculiaremque parochum assignent,"* words which surely argue that the requirements of the law were that the pastor be perpetual. Nor does the phrase immediately following, *"aut alio utiliori modo prout loci qualitas exegerit, provideant,"* militate against the necessity of stability as demanded in the preceding phrase, because these words may have reference to the establishment of parishes in other ways than that which the preceding words demanded, as well as to the perpetuity of the pastor.

In many decisions, especially of the Sacred Congregation of the Council, the Church has plainly manifested that it is her mind that all pastors should be permanently established in their parishes.[11]

One might here object that, even if it were granted that the

---

[9] Syn. Placentinae, 1095, Can. 15; cf. c. 2, D. 70; also 2-4, X, III, 5; Conc. Londoniense, 1125, c. 8; Mansi, XXI, 331.

[10] Claeys-Bouuaert, 286.

[11] Claeys-Bouuaert, 296-30, who also gives references to the decision in other authors. For the arguments of those Canonists who hold that stability is not necessary for the pastoral office and that removability can be justified according to Church legislation; cf. Claeys-Bouuaert, 297, who answers these arguments on page 302; Bouix, De Parocho, 192-213, Bargilliat, Praelect, Juris Canon, 24 ed., II, §1012; Boudinhon, Inamovabilite, 6; Nardi, Dei Parochi I, 480; Vacandard-Mangenot, Dict. col., 2440, §2; Smith, elements of Ecc. law, I, 373, §643.

mind of the Church has been that pastors should be irremovable, has she not contradicted this doctrine, especially during the past century, in permitting the wide-spread rise of removable parishes in many European countries, and particularly in France and the United States? To this objection the answer can be given that this abnormal state of affairs has been tolerated by the Church, because of the circumstances which demanded it, and in no way argues that she had changed her traditional position regarding the stability of the pastoral office. If one considers the reasons why the Church tolerated and even tacitly consented to this wide spread rise of removable pastors in the last century, the force of this answer would become evident.

Whatever may have been the reasons for the existence of pastors removable at will by the bishops, it can be safely asserted that wherever such pastors did exist, as soon as circumstances permitted, attempts were made to make at least a certain percentage of them irremovable. This fact shows that the mind of the Church has always been that pastors be permanently established in their parishes.[12]

Another question much discussed by canonists is in regard to the manner and reason for the removal of pastors *"ad nutum."* Was a canonical trial, either solemn or summary, required for the removal of such pastors, or could they be removed without any further trial at all? Again, was a canonical cause necessary for such removal, or could these pastors be removed for any reason judged sufficient by the bishop or even without any reason at all.[13]

---

[12] Cf. Bouix, De Parocho, 220-242; Bargilliat, Praelect. Juris Can., 24 ed., I, sec. 1015; Boudinhon, Inamovabilite, II; Vacandard-Mangenot, Dict. col., 2440, n. 10 Claeys-Bouuaert, De Can. Cleri Saec. obed., 304; Ayrinhac, Const. of Church, 298; A. A. S., XIV, 181; Canon Contemp. V, 5.

[13] Cf. Bouix, De Parocho, 398-414, where may be found the teaching of the canonists such as Suarez, Garcias, Lotterus, Gonzalez, De Luca, and Leurenius, Bargilliat, Praelect, Jus. Can., 24 ed., II sec., 1017; Boudinhon, Inamovabilite des desservants, 7 and 14; Claeys-Bouuaert, De Canon. Cleri. Saec. Obed., 300. After giving the opinion of some of the older canonists and several decisions of the S. C. of the Council, he treats fully the question of the removability of the *"desservants"* in France, proving from many decisions of the Holy See that their status was no different from that of the pastors *"amovibiles ad nutum."* Wernz, Jus. Decret. II, sec. 826; Boriero, Manuale per Processo Canonico, 404, footnote 2; Smith, Elements of Ecc. Law, I, p. 178, sec. 418; Smith, New Procedure, etc., 248, sec. 586; Baart, Legal Formulary, p. 470, sec. 536; Sebastianelli, apud Analacta Ecclesiastica, IV, 83; A. A. S., III, 560; XII, p. 283.

Whatever may have been the opinion of canonists in the past, this question was definitely settled by the decree, "*Maxima Cura,*" which, though it did not entirely destroy the class of removable pastors did away with the removability "*ad nutum,*" when it demanded definite reasons and a mode of procedure. Thus it prescribed, "*Superius constitutis regulis . . . adamussim applicandis iis omnibus qui paroeciam, quovis titulo, ut proprii ejus rectores obtinent, sive nuncupentur Vicarii, sive desservantes, sive alio quolivet nomine.*" Too much stress, however, cannot be laid on the application of this document to the United States. The purpose of the decree "*Maxima Cura*" was not so much to change the status of removable pastors as to make more easy the removal of irremovable pastors. It introduced the administrative removal for these latter and did away with the necessity of the former solemn or summary procedure for such cases. The principle of the decree is, "*salus animarim, suprema lex.*" Some thought that the decree of 1910 affected the movable pastors in this country also, since the United States had been taken away from the Congregation of the Propaganda by the decree of 1908, "*Sapienti Consilio,*" and put under the common law of the Church. But such was not the case, for on June 28, 1915, the Consistorial Congregation declared that the decree of Pius X, "*Maxima Cura,*" did not give greater permanency to the movable pastors of parishes in the United States. They still remained the vicars of the Ordinary. The "*dubium*" proposed to Consistorial Congregation at the time was as follows: "*Utrum in Foederatis Americae Statibus rectores paroeciarum seu Missionum, qui inter inamovibiles juxta Concilium Baltimorense III, non recensentur, se adhuc amovibiles nuncupantur, vi decreti, solummodo amoveri seu transferri possint, servato ordine processus in memorato decreto statuti, in generali conventu diei 28 Junii 1915, Emi. S. C. Patres, visis consultorum votis et quaestione rite discussa, respondendum censuerunt; Negative; Sed amoveri posse ad nutum episcopi, firmo tamen monito Concilii Baltimorensis II, ne episcopi hoc jure suo, nisi graves ob causas et habita meritorum uti velint.* So that after the decree "*Maxima Cura*" of 1910, the removability "*of the parochi amovibiles*" remained just what it had been before. Hence, prescinding from the irremovable pastors who were appointed through the concursus, all other pastors of this country were "*amovibiles ad nutum,*" until the publication of the Code in 1918.

CHAPTER XVII

The Stability of Pastors in the Code

The Code of Canon Law resting on the traditional teaching as already shown, has decreed, *"Qui paroeciae administrandae praeficiuntur qua proprii ejusdem rectores, stabiles in ea esse debent, quod tamen non impedit quominus omnes ab eis removeri queant ad normam juris."* In this stability, degrees are to be distinguished, for the same canon continues, *"At non omnes parochi eandem obtinent stabilitatem; qui majore guadent, inamovibiles, qui minore, amovibiles appellari solent."* [1] Hence except in the case of *"quasi parochi,"* and religious pastors, the Code practically abolished removability *"ad nutum"* as had been decreed in the *"Maxima Cura."* All pastors henceforth must be removed according to process of law.

Before going any further into the explanation of this canon, a comparison should be made with the ruling of the Third Plenary Council of Baltimore. The status of the pastor at present is somewhat different than it was at that time. In fact it might truthfully be stated that the ruling of the Council of Baltimore on this point has been abrogated. First of all the present legislator does not impose the nomenclature of irremovable and removable as permanently technical and definite, for he uses the expression, *"appellari solent,"* i. e., as they are usually denoted. But the meaning which he gives to these old terms is entirely new. In the old law removable meant *"ad nutum,"* and irremovable meant those who had been appointed by means of the concursus, and who could not very easily be removed. The one was almost the contradiction of the other. Not so for the future. Removable pastors, as well as irremovable ones henceforth, are removable only according to process of the law, for specified reasons. No pastor is to be considered as *"ad*

---

[1] Cf. cc. 454, §1, §2.

nutum" removable. The Church has always abhorred the expression *"ab arbitrio,"* and now since the exigency calling for the *"ad nutum"* action of the Ordinary in this matter has to her mind passed for such countries as this, where the missionary status has been changed, she directs that the common law of the Church on the point of parishes be carried out fully, as it is elsewhere.

Practically what does this mean for the pastor under present conditions? It means that the bishop should consult the desires of the incumbent of a parish before removing him, if there can be no devised reason for a removal. Not that the bishop's hands are tied in this respect as to the governing of his diocese, for if the reasonable cause be at hand, and this is derived from the *welfare of souls, which is the supreme law,* and the good of the diocese, he can always take that action which he deems wisest.[2] But in what does this stability mentioned in the new law consist? It consists in this that canonical procedure is involved in all removals and that the degree of the removability is determined by the process of removal. By the decree *"Maxima Cura,"* the removal of irremovable pastors was expedited inasmuch as the administrative removal did away with the solemn process which previously had applied to all forms of removal of *irremovables.* It must be understood that the criminal procedure is not being discussed here. Now then in the later legislation, a procedure is prescribed for the removal of removable pastors.

Until 1918, all the pastors of the United States who were not permanent rectors could be taken away from their parishes if the bishop so willed. With the promulgation of the Code, not only is this ruling abolished,[3] but all customs contrary to the recent ruling are suppressed. *"Non obstantibus quibuslibet ordinationibus, constitutionibus privilegiis etiam speciali atque individua mentione dignis, necnon consuetudinibus etiam immemorabilibus ceterisque contrariis quibusvis."* [4] Further it must be concluded that from now on, no one is justified in following earlier legislation which is contrary to the Code.[5]

---

[2] Cf. Canon 2147, 2157.

[3] This was the case even after 1908—for this country. Cf. A. A. S., 1915.

[4] Cf. Constitutio Apostolica, *"Providentissima Mater Ecclesia"* at the beginning of the Code.

[5] Cf. Can. 6, §1, and also Can. 5.

This change has been made in the favor of the pastor, as the Church has always recognized that he could perform his ministry much more fruitfully, if he felt secure in his parish. Free from the fear that he can be disturbed by his Ordinary as long as there is no justifiable complaint against him, he can give himself whole-heartedly to his *care of souls* as his lifetime work. So that, as long as he puts his soul into his charge he can remain where he is, provided always that in the good judgment of his superior his apostolic services are not in greater demand elsewhere. Such discipline marks a very important progress for the Church in this country.

Mention was made of criminal or penal removal. One cannot say simply that the greater or lesser facility with which the pastor can be removed or transferred, determines the degree of stability, so that the irremovable and movable pastors do not differ as to judicial or penal privation.[6] Yet this is true in a certain sense. In the case of administrative removal or transfer, though the same reasons are applicable to both irremovable and movable pastors, still in the case of the latter a more simple form of procedure is permitted. They do differ as to penal removal, for otherwise one must admit that the same definite reasons mentioned in the Code and the same judicial process is required for the privation of a removable parish as for an irremovable one. This is not true. A removable pastor differs from a irremovable one also as regards penal removal,[7] because the former can be deprived of his benefice in punishment for any reasonable cause other than that mentioned in law, and without the observance of any canonical trial, for at most the procedure employed is the administrative removal.[8] Aside from the fact that the process of removal for removable pastors is slightly easier and shorter than that of irremovable pastors, there is no difference between the two in the respect of removal. Concerning transfer, they differ in this, that the irremovable pastor cannot be transferred if he is unwilling (*invitus*) without a special permission of the Holy See, while the removable pastor can be

[6] Cf. Ayrinhac, Constitution of the Church, p. 315, sec. 256.

[7] Cf. cc. 192, §3; 2299, §1; Vermeersch-Creusen, Epit., III, No. 497; Cocchi, De Parochis, p. 385, gives as the causes of removal the five mentioned in Canon 2147, §2. Cf. cc. 2147-2153 and 2157-2161. Cf. cc. 192, §3; 2299, §1.

[8] Cf. Can. 192, §3; 2299, §1; Vermeersch-Creusen, Epit. III, 252, §497.

sent to another parish even when unwilling. Another difference between the two is that the irremovable rectors are all to be consulted by the bishop concerning those priests whose names he desires to suggest at the annual meeting of the bishops of the province, as being *"episcopabiles."* [9] Care must be taken to realize that according to modern legislation, administrative removals are not in the way of punishment. It is an administrative act of the Bishop induced by the consideration of the welfare of souls and the good of the diocese.

I. *The Sources of Stability*

The positive legislation of the Code is the reason for the stability of pastors. The effective cause (*causa effectiva*) is undoubtedly the appointment of the Bishop, i. e., the decree of appointment. Indirectly, of course, stability comes from the *title* which in turn is conferred by the Bishop.[10] An office is called irremovable if once entrusted to a person it cannot be withdrawn unless by process of law.[11] Essentially then irremovability does not pertain to the parochial office as there can exist parishes that are removable. For the office of the pastor is, that he is bound in his own name to exercise the care of souls over a certain distinct part of a diocese. Irremovability in that office is derived from the sacred canons and especially from the Code of 1918. It is not derived from the fact that all the parishes in this country are benefices. Logically, the parochial office's permanency is prior to the fact that the parish is a perpetual benefice. This fact does make for permanency, but it is not the source from which the canonical pastors at present derive their irremovability.

According to Canon 1438 all secular benefices (parochial and otherwise) should be conferred for life, unless the law of foundation of the benefice, or a particular indult or an immemorial custom permit otherwise. Even then a parochial benefice may lack objective perpetuity. Therefore parochial benefices should be conferred with subjective perpetuity whether the pastor be

---

[9] Decree of S. Cong. Consistorialis, concerning the election of bishops in the United States; cf. A. A. S., VII, 1916.

[10] Cf. 451, §1.

[11] Cf. Bouix, o. c., par. I, sec. II, cap. 3.

removable or irremovable.[12] It is this subjective perpetuity which the Code confers in this canon on the stability of pastors. So then all parochial benefices of this country are perpetual whether the pastor be called removable or irremovable.[13] When the Code says that all secular benefices should be conferred for life (*ad vitam*) the rule is carried out by conferring this subjective perpetuity on the incumbents of canonical parishes. But none the less when necessity arises the law allows the Bishop to promote the welfare of his diocese by removing or transferring these perpetual beneficiaries, with the exception of the *unwilling irremovable pastor.* In all cases the welfare of souls is the supreme law and rises above every circumstance. The reasons for removal are expressed in the law and must always be borne in mind; so that all pastors are in reality perpetual and cannot be removed otherwise than as just mentioned,[14] except when necessity which is supposed to know no law, demands.

The law says that all secular benefices are perpetual unless immemorial custom permit otherwise. Some may claim that here is an immemorial custom for the removable (*"ad nutum"*) parishes in this country, but it does not seem that such a custom may be alleged. For in its missionary state this country had no parishes in the canonical sense, and therefore no custom to the contrary could have originated with regard to canonical parishes that did not exist. Our parishes are in a new state, and any custom to the contrary must arise in the future (i. e., after 1918). Furthermore all existing custom which is contrary to the present law, was suppressed by the promulgation of the Code according to Canon 5. The new law says that a particular indult may permit secular benefices to be conferred otherwise

---

[12] Cf. Canon 145, §1: Officium Ecclesiasticum . . . Stricte Autem sensu est munus Ordinatione sive divina sive ecclesiastica stabiliter constitutum, ad sacrorum canonum conferendum.

[13] Cf. Canon 1438.

[14] 1. Imperitia vel permanens infirmitas mentis aut corporis . . . si per vicarium adiutorem provideri nequeat;

2. Odium plebis, quamvis injustum et non universale . . . quod utile parochi ministerium impediat, nec brevi cessaturum praevideatur;

3. Bonae existimationis amissio penes probos et graves viros;

4. Mala rerum temporalium administratio cum gravi ecclesiae aut beneficii damno, si huic remedium afferri nequeat. Modus autem servandus in remotione traditur in tit. XXVII pro parochis inamovibilibus; in tit. XXVIII pro parochis amovibilibus.

than as subjectively perpetual. An example of this was the indult obtained by the Plenary Council of Latin America in 1899, to appoint to canonical parishes with a revocable *"ad nutum"* title. But as far as is known to the writer no such indult has been obtained by any Bishop of this country since the Code of 1918.

The law of foundation of benefices may also provide that the pastor be removable *"ad nutum."* Canon 1417 says that in founding a benefice, the founder may, with the consent of the Ordinary place conditions which are contrary to common law provided that they be honorable and are not contrary to the nature of benefices. To place such a condition on a subjective tenure could be allowed, and once admitted would compel the Ordinary to give such a benefice with a revocable title. The erection of this sort of benefice with this consideration granted the founder, refers to *"juspatronatus"* which is frowned upon by the Code. The founders of benefices are invited to renounce the right of patronage. Needless to say no such parish is found in this country.

II. *The Stability of the Religious Pastor*

The exact contrary of the above rule of stability of secular pastors is true with regard to religious pastors as they are removable at the will either of the Bishop or the religious Superior. When the Superior finds it advisable to remove his subject from the position of shepherd of a flock, he simply notifies the Ordinary of his intention without asking any permission or even consent for his action. The removal then is valid. The Ordinary in like manner may notify the religious Superior of his intention to remove the head of the religious parish without asking the Superior's permission or even consent. In both cases neither the Ordinary nor the religious Superior is held to explain one to the other, the reason for his decision. But in either case recourse *"in devolutivo"* to the Apostolic See is granted. This means that if the Ordinary or the religious Superior objects to the proposed removal of the *"de facto"* holder of the parish, the religious pastor loses the possession of the parish, and the case is settled by the Holy See.

The reason for not making a religious pastor permanent, is

that he is bound by the vow of obedience to go wherever he is sent, and the obtaining of a permanent benefice would seriously endanger the observance of his vow. It has been remarked in the historical discussion of this essay that the same view cannot be taken of the promise of obedience which the newly ordained priest makes to his Bishop or Ordinary on the day of his ordination. For the Sacred Congregation of the Propaganda of June 30, 1831, in correcting the decrees of the First Synod of Baltimore (1829-1831) stated that pastors in the United States were movable *"ad nutum"* according to the ruling of Benedict XIV, not by virtue of the solemn promise of obedience made at ordination. They advised the Bishops of the United States to counsel their priests to keep this promise constantly in mind with regard to their appointments.

III. *Stability of Parishes*

The mind of the Church, namely, that all parishes should be irremovable is clearly implied in §3 of Canon 454. For this canon regulates not only that all parishes which became irremovable according to the ruling of the Third Plenary Council of Baltimore, must remain so; but also that all new parishes to be erected are to be considered as irremovable with the exception described in two paragraphs further on. First, that all of the parishes that were formerly irremovable by virtue of the legislation of the Council of Baltimore must remain so is the unmistakable meaning of this new law, follows from the statement that irremovable parishes cannot without the expressed permission of the Holy See (*sine beneplacito Apostolico*) be reduced to the state of removable rectorships. This we know for a certainty that in one of the Archdioceses of this country the Ordinary obtained the permission from Rome to reduce the number of irremovable rectorships in his Archdiocese.

Removable parishes can by the Bishop and by him alone be declared irremovable. This declaration cannot be made by the Vicar Capitular or Administrator (*sede vacante*) even with the advice of the Cathedral Chapter or the *"coetus consultorum."* This does not at all seem strange, since in a preceding chapter a quotation was given from a letter of a former Apostolic Delegate to the Bishops of this country dated 1922 (consequently since the Code) which inculcated the understanding that those parishes which prior to the Code had been erected whether removable or irremovable automatically became canonical parishes and therefore benefices. The Code as well as previous legislation desires that all secular benefices be permanent or perpetual.[15] Without then imposing upon the Ordinary the obligation of changing all the removable pastorates into irremovables, the Church prepares the way for him to do so with great facility. Though she does not exhort him to do so directly, at least indirectly she seems to desire it by reason of the fact that there is practically no formality beyond that of the declaration required for this act.

The desire of the Church for irremovability in all parishes is further deduced from this, that she lays down the ruling that all future parishes (i. e., after 1918) to be erected, are to be taken as irremovable unless the Bishop finds that the circumstances of the place or of the people demand that they should be removable. In order to form this judgment more safely, he should consult the chapter (or "*coetus consultorum*") (*audito Capitulo*). The erection must be made by a public decree (*publicum instrumentum*). The rule may be formulated as follows: In general all new parishes are to be irremovable with the exception of those for which the peculiar conditions or people do not warrant the character of irremovability. Thus a Bishop cannot express the general intention of erecting none but removable parishes. Irremovability is to be the rule, removability, the exception. The exception depends on the persons and places, each instance considered in particular. Are they such that the Bishop has a sufficient reason for creating a parish otherwise than endowed with the characteristic of irremovability? The question is to be decided by the consideration of expediency (*magis expedire*). It may so happen that a Bishop has as part of his diocese a district of which the population is very unstable and fluctuating, and owing to this fact conditions do not warrant that a newly created parish be given the same degree of stability as those erected in more flourishing parts of the diocese.

Before concluding this chapter a word must be said of "*quasi-parochi*" and those who are in charge of "*quasi-paroeciae.*"

---

[15] Cf. Can. 1438.

Quasi-parishes are those divisions of Vicariates and Prefectures Apostolic which correspond to the territorial divisions into parishes of regularly constituted dioceses. The pastors of these *quasi-parishes* are called *quasi-pastors* and are, all of them, removable *"ad nutum,"* for the word removable as used in this particular canon is in no way modified and consequently is taken in the sense of movable *"ad nutum"* in contradistinction to the expression movable *"ad normam juris,"* which is the prerogative of pastors of canonical parishes. *Quasi-pastors* and *quasi-parishes* are not *pastors* nor *parishes* in a *canonical* sense and do not enjoy this same degree of stability.

CHAPTER XVIII

The Conferring of Parishes

Canon 455

§1. Ius nominandi et instituendi parochos competit Ordinario loci, exceptis paroeciis Sanctae Sedi reservatis, reprobata contraria consuetudine, sed salvo privilegio electionis aut praesentationis, si cui legitime competat.

§2. Sede vacante aut impedita ad normam Can. 429, ad Vicarium Capitularem aliumve qui dioecesim regat, pertinent:

1°. Vicarios paroeciales constitutere ad normam Can. 472-476;
2°. Confirmare electionem aut acceptare presentationem ad paroeciam vacantem, et institutionem electo aut praesentato concedere;
3°. Paroeciae liberae collationis conferre, si sedes ab anno saltem vacaverit.

§3. Horum nihil Vicario Generali competit sine mandato speciali, salvo praescripto cit. Can. 429, par. 1.

I. *Sede Plena*

With the exception of those parishes reserved to the Holy See and those which have the privilege of election or presentation, the right of appointing and investing the parish Priest belongs to the Ordinary of the diocese. All contrary customs are hereby explicitly rejected (*reprobata contraria consuetudine*). This means that the Bishop, even before his consecration,[1] provided he has presented his Apostolic Letters of promotion to the See, to the Cathedral Chapter (or to the administrator),

[1] Cf. Can. 334, §3.

is the Ordinary and only one to confer all benefices in his diocese excepting the reserved, or disputed ones.[2] He has this prerogative by law and enjoys the favor of law. This power flows naturally from his office as chief Pastor of the whole district by virtue of which he is obliged to provide for the spiritual welfare of all the people of the whole diocese. It were impossible for him to accomplish this important task unaided. For this reason, the Council of Trent laid on all Bishops the duty of portioning their dioceses into districts called parishes, each with its own peculiar and proper Pastor.

The principle of law is that *"ex jure et per se,"* no one can validly make provision for an ecclesiastical office unless he possesses competent ecclesiastical authority. For those things which by their very nature pertain to the Church are governed *"per se"* by ecclesiastical authority. Wherefore neither the Christian people nor civil government have any power in this matter; and if at any time they have had a say in the appointments to ecclesiastical offices, it was by special privileges, in the way of election, patronage or concordat agreements.

There is a corollary which flows from this principle embodied in Canon 1437, viz., that no one can confer a benefice on himself.[3] This prohibition is similar to the one recorded in Canon 170, which says that no one can validly vote for himself. The Bishop cannot therefore acquire for himself any of the vacant benefices of his diocese.

As regards civil law, the civil courts of this country have no power to control the appointments of a religious society in the employment and payment of a minister.[4] This is the general rule. Consequently it has been decided in more than one case, "By the Laws and customs of the Roman Catholic Church in the United States, a Priest is liable to be removed from the charge of a congregation at the pleasure of the Bishop . . ." "The Pastoral relations are neither created nor dissolved by agreements between the priest and the congregation; and the Bishop appoints or removes the shepherd as he deems fit

[2] Cf. Pius IX Const. "Rom. Pontifex," Aug. 28, 1873, Fontes 565; Const. "Apostolicae Sedis," Oct. 12, 1869, Fontes 552; S. d'Angelo, Parroco E Parrochia, p. 47, II, Vescovi.

[3] Cf. Can. 2394.

[4] Cf. C. Z. Lincoln, The Civil Law and The Church, 1916, p. 156.

for the Priest's good or the interest of the flock." "Removal is the exercise of a Episcopal authority according to the Bishop's judgment."[5]

II. *Reservations*

The Pope being the Pastor of Pastors, as head of the universal Church possesses the plenitude of power and jurisdiction over the whole Church, and consequently can appoint any Pastor to any Church in the whole world. As a matter of expediency he usually does not exercise this prerogative to a very great extent. Yet, in time past this power was claimed and exercised by the Roman Pontiff very extensively during the Avignon period (1304-1378). The principle of reservation had been emphatically asserted already in the Decretal of Clement IV.[6] This decretal mentioned as reserved to the Apostolic See parishes or benefices which become vacant at the Apostolic See. The explanation of this expression has been given in the historical section of this thesis.[*] Therefore, in the cases referred to, the Pope and not the Ordinary was to fill the vacancy. This law was adopted as a rule (*prima*) of the Apostolic Chancery. It may be permitted to add the law laid down in the decretal, and the first rule of the Chancery were never applied to this country. The question is, do the reservations mentioned in the Code of 1918 now apply to this country?

According to the Code a parish may be reserved to the Holy See in one of the following four ways; first, *"Jure praeventionis," "jure concursus," "jure devolutionis,"* and *"jure reservationis."* In Canon 1431, the stipulation is made that the Roman Pontiff has a right to confer all benefices throughout the whole Church and to reserve to himself the conferring of the same. Thus the Pope could appoint to any parish anywhere, at any time, Pastors to fill a vacancy. More than this he could appoint coadjutors with the right of succession even before the parish became vacant. According to Canon 1432 §3, if the Ordinary through negligence or any other culpability does not confer a benefice

[5] Stack v. O'Hara, 98 Pa., 213, Lincoln, l. c. p., 679.

[6] Cf. c. 2, III, 4 in VI°: Concerning the historical parts, Cf. Scherer, I, 1283; Wernz, Jus Decretalium, I, ed. II, p. 448, ff., Sagmueller, p. 272; Bouix, De Parocho, p. 310 seqq.

[*] Cf. chap. XII.

within six months after learning of the vacancy the filling of the vacancy devolves upon the Holy See (*salvo praescripto* Can. 458, which shall be seen later). The following benefices, by the ruling of Canon 1435 are reserved to the Holy See: All those to which the care of souls is attached, becoming vacant through the death, promotion, renunciation or translation, of a Cardinal, a Legate of the Roman Pontiff, major officials of the Sacred Congregations, of the tribunal and offices of the Roman curia and of the Familiares (Domestic Prelates, Monsignori,[7] etc., even though they be merely honorary) of the Supreme Pontiff at the time of the vacancy. Also the papal reservations affect those founded outside the Roman curia, which become vacant by the death of the beneficiary in the City of Rome itself. Another class of reserved benefices consists of those which have been invalidly conferred because of simony. Finally, benefices are reserved on which the Roman Pontiff has placed his hands himself or through a delegate in one of the following manners: If the election to the benefice had been rescinded by the Pope, or the electors were forbidden by the Pope to proceed with the election; or if the beneficiary had been promoted, transferred, or deprived of his benefice by the Pope or finally if he had received his benefice (*in commendam*) from the Pope himself.[8]

The question arises, it may be repeated, whether Papal and other reservations are going to be applied to this country in the strict form in which they are put forth by the Code. Augustine and others seem to be of the opinion that the United States will be exempt from such a complication of the universal law of the Church. It seems, however, that the question is one on which custom will decide a great deal for the future. There are certain facts which seem to indicate that at least some of the reservations of parishes contained in the Code may be applicable to this country. For instance, in the Bulls of Appointment of several of the recently made auxiliary Bishops, a phrase was contained designating the fact that the parishes of which they had been Pastors were now declared vacant and reserved to the Holy See. It has been impossible to get exact information about all of the Episcopal Appointments since the publication of the

---

[7] Cf. Pistocchi, De Re Beneficiati, p. 185.
[8] Rossi, De Paroecia, pp. 145, 146.

Code.* It is to be presumed that the policy followed by the Holy See in one instance does not differ from that of the others. In one instance the writer has *certain knowledge* that an Ordinary of a large diocese in which there has been recently appointed an Auxiliary applied to Rome to know, if this Auxiliary whose parish had thus been declared vacant, could still retain his office as Pastor. The answer of the Holy See was to the effect that in the case, the Ordinary could leave the Auxiliary in the office of Pastor of that particular parish despite the clause of reservation in his Bull of Appointments as Bishop.[9] Should it be said that Rome is granting a sort of dispensation or "sanatio" for these individual cases, or can one go further and state that by giving this permission to the Ordinary in the matter, Rome is giving tacit consent to the starting of a custom contrary to the legislation in the Code of Canon Law on the reservation of parishes and benefices? It seems more probable that in the cases of promotion to the episcopacy, those parishes are reserved whose incumbents are promoted.

Another case of reservation mentioned in the Code is to be found in Canon 274 §1. If a Suffragan, unhindered by just impediment, fails within the time specified by law, to institute those presented by patrons for benefices of *"juspatronatus,"* the Metropolitan can make the institution. *A pari* if a Metropolitan fail in a similar case, the devolution goes back to the Pope.† This is likewise the consequence if a Bishop is directly subject

---

* The writer has *certain information,* that in the cases of such promotions during the last three years, the parishes were reserved.

[9] S. C. C. Decretum 367/25 Cum. R. P. D. . . . iam parochus ecclesiae . . . in civitate . . . nupperime ad dignitatem Episcopi . . . et simul . . . evectus sit: S. Congregatio Consistorialis, benigne annuens precibus ab ipso Revmo Archiepiscopo porrectis, indulget ut, *tanquam non apposita in Bullis Pontificiis habeatur clausula de vacatione et reservatione beneficii* ab Electo possessi, ideoque ipse beneficium idem retinere valeat. Contrariis quibuscumque non obstantibus. Datum Romae, ex aedibus S. C. C. . . . The expression "benigne annuens precibus" is explained by a letter written by a member of the Congregation in Italian to the Archbishop. S. C. C. Num Di Prot. 967/25. La S. C. *trova molto giuste le ragione addotte* dalla S. V. Revma per laciare Mons . . . electto suo Vescovo Ausiliare, al posto to di parroco. This seems to imply that the decree furnishes an exception to the rule. Cf., also The Faculties of the Apostolic Delegate—Caput I, §3—quoted by Vermeersch-Creusen, Epit. I, p. 523; conferendi personis dignis ea beneficia, de quibus in Canon 1435, §1 and §3, Servatis regulis ab ap. Dataria datis vel dandis.

† Cf. Maroto, Institutiones Juris Canonici, I, p. 691, *b*.

to the Apostolic See.[10] As far as is known *"juspatronatus"* is practically a nonentity in this country; therefore a further discussion is unnecessary.

III. *Election and Presentation*

It seems according to certain authors that the right of popular election to parishes is enjoyed in certain countries by certain people. Several authors refer to this fact, but no quotation is given of an authentic document to substantiate their claim. It may be that this privilege is based on ancient custom. Augustine in his commentary claims that in some parts of Switzerland Pastors are chosen by the popular election of the parishioners, the selection being made by majority count.[11] Ayrinhac on the contrary says that attempts made in the last century, to give the election of pastors to their parishioners, in Italy, Switzerland and Prussia met with prompt rebuke from Rome.[12] Does the Code safeguard this right in Switzerland as Augustine infers? Godfrey informs us on page 55 of his dissertation, "In many countries, e. g., in the kingdom of Venice, in parts of Austria, Germany and Switzerland,[13] presentations to churches are made by means of popular election. That is, a body of the faithful, such as a congregation, or a town, possesses collectively the rights to present rectors and pastors to vacant benefices and parochial churches." Such presentations have grown up by custom or prescription,[14] and were not sanctioned by the common law of the Church even before the Code. Now by the new legislation they are tolerated but only restrictedly, viz.: "Popular election and presentation to benefices, even to parochial ones can be tolerated wherever they exist, only when the people choose one priest among three designated by the Ordinary of the place."[15] If a concursus has been held for the vacant

---

[10] Cf. Canon 274, §1.

[11] Cf. Augustine, vol. II, p. 524; Wernz, II, n. 287 (p. 393, ed. 1).

[12] Cf. Ayrinhac, Const. of the Church, p. 319; Pius IX, Const. "Etsi Multa," Nov. 21, 1873, Fontes, 566.

[13] Cf. A. A. S. XIII, 163. This document referred to by Godfrey concerns a special case of *juspatronatus* in which no mention is made of the countries he enumerates; Augustine, VI, 526.

[14] Cf. Blat. III, p. 356.

[15] Cf. Can. 1452. Cf. Godfrey, Right of Patronage, p. 141.

benefice, one of those must be chosen who have been approved in the concursus. Here it seems that the Ordinary allows those who enjoy this privilege of election to choose only from the three candidates whom he selects.

In some countries such as in Spain by a concordat, the civil government has some part in the appointment of Pastors. This is allowed by special agreement between the Holy See and the government itself. In these instances those elected or presented where this privilege is enforced, need Episcopal institution or investiture, i. e., the express judgment of the Ordinary that the candidate is fit, and the formal bestowal of the parochial right by the Ordinary.

Another mode of restriction on the free power of the Bishop to appoint incumbents to the parishes of his dioceses is that they are presented to him by a person whether moral or physical enjoying the privilege of presentation. Though this privilege is applicable to this country only in part, yet a word should be said in passing concerning it. As to *"juspatronatus,"* it must be borne in mind that the Church desires to abolish it as well as the right of election. It does not take away the already existing privileges in these respects, but it does invite those who have used them to renounce them. In the future they will probably be avoided as they are onerous. By presentation the Code includes also the right of a religious community or institute to present to the Ordinary the appointee for a vacant religious parish, whether it be united *"pleno jure"* or *"semi-pleno jure"* to the religious community. Be it remembered that in the event that a concursus has been held for a vacant benefice, only those who have been approved in the concursus may be presented to the Ordinary for institution.

The Vicar General has no power to appoint or to approve one elected or presented for the parochial office without a special mandate. This mandate is not general, but is special for each individual case. The mandate must be in writing. Then in the particular instance he acts as *"mandatarius"* and not merely as *"executor."*

IV. *Religious Parishes and Quasi-Parishes*

Canon 456

Ad paroecias religiosis concreditas Superior, cui ex constitutionibus id competit, sacerdotem suae religionis praesentat Ordinario loci; qui eidem, servato praescripto Can. 459, §2, institutionem concedit.

Canon 457

Quasi-parochos e clero saeculari proprius loci Ordinarius nominat, audito Consilio de quo in Can. 302.

On Canon 456 it is not necessary to go into great detail, as this essay does not purport to treat extensively the question of religious. That question would involve a rather longer explanation than we have the space and time for here. Accordingly then, it is ordained that for parishes entrusted to religious orders and institutes, the respective superior who exercises the right under the constitution, shall present a *Priest* of his community to the Ordinary of the diocese who shall in turn invest him conformably to Canon 459 §2. The religious superior himself cannot be at the same time the Pastor.[16] This canon does not distinguish between a parish incorporated with a religious community *"pleno jure"* or only *"semi-pleno jure"* but employs the general term, *"ad paroecias religiosis concreditas,"* [17] and hence both kinds are understood. It must be remarked that parishes united *"semi-pleno jure,"* i. e., for temporalities only, are not religious parishes properly so-called, but secular parishes. Wherefore it would seem that the Superior should present a *secular* priest. In this case, the one appointed is rather a

---

[16] Cf. cc. 1478, 471, §4; Blat., II, 484; Interdictum, May 28, 1845. Even if the religious house be attached to the Church, the religious superior cannot be pastor.

[17] In speaking of parishes joined to Religious orders or communities the Code uses two terms, *"Concreditae"* and *"unitae."* Before the Code the expression *"incorporatae"* was used. *"Unitae"* seems to refer to *"pleno jure unitae"*; *"concreditae"* is broader, and includes all sorts of union; *"semi-pleno"* as well as *"pleno jure,"* even if the parish be entrusted only temporarily to the religious.

"parochus" than a *"vicarius perpetuus,"* and is not to be removed *"ad nutum."* How then explain *"sacerdos suae religionis?"* It is hard to ascertain the specific meaning of the word *"Concreditas religiosis"* as used here and elsewhere in the Code. Presentation by the Superior is mentioned as a *"conditio sine qua non."*

Generally speaking, the word superior is understood as embracing all those who are known as major superiors.[18] The candidate presented must be a *Priest* endowed with all the qualities required in a *"parochus."* Therefore, this canon refers to Canon 459 §2, where the Bishop is called upon to judge the ability of the candidate presented by the religious superior, not the learning only, but also the other qualities. Would not then the Bishop be justified in requiring an examination as to the fitness of the candidate presented? Naturally, if the Bishop is morally certain as to the candidate's qualifications, he need not subject him to an examination. Once the candidate is found fit by the Bishop, he is bound to give him investiture.[19]

Under Canon 457 come Vicariates and Prefectures Apostolic. In them the parishes are all *quasi-parishes,* and therefore the Pastors are without exception movable *"ad nutum."* The prefect or the Vicar Apostolic *even though he has not the episcopal character,*[20] is the Ordinary of the place, and he it is who makes all appointments in his territory. He must first have the advice of his counsel or at least three of his older and more experienced missionaries, according to Canon 302. This advice must be taken *at least by letter.* This summary information is sufficient for our purpose, lest we digress too far from our main subject.

V. *Sede Vacante Aut Impedita*

According to Canons 429 and 430, an Episcopal See becomes impeded in the legal sense of the term, when its incumbent, whilst retaining the title, cannot discharge the function of the office, owing to either a physical or canonical obstacle. The physical impediments are those which prevent him from ruling

[18] Cf. c. 488, §8.

[19] Cf. cc. 177, 1466; Conc. Trid. Sess., 25, c. 11, de reg.; Pius V, "Ad exequendum," §4; Bull, Rom. IV, 11, 402; Piatus Mont., Praelect. Juris reg. ed. 2, II, p. 20. Even a religious superior though a prelate may be subjected to an examination, S. C. C., Jan. 7, 1775; Piatus Mont., l. c.

[20] Cf. Canon 294, §2.

his diocese and even communicating by letter with his subjects, such as captivity, whether in the hands of pagans, heretics, schismatics, external enemies, internal foes or fellow-citizens; relegation or exclusion from the diocese, exile, inability, whether due to bodily or mental infirmity, culpable or inculpable. By canonical law a Bishop becomes unable to rule his diocese and exercise jurisdiction if he falls under a declaratory sentence of excommunication, interdict, or suspension.

An Episcopal See becomes vacant when the incumbent ceases to hold the title or to be really its Bishop. This may occur by death, resignation duly accepted by the Sovereign Pontiff, by legitimate transfer and by privation of office pronounced in legal form.[21]

In the case of an impeded See the Vicar Capitular or Administrator,[22] unless the Holy See has provided otherwise, is entitled to appoint temporary vicars or assistants to vacant parishes and to grant investiture to such as are elected or presented. When the See is vacant in the case of *"libera collatio"* which belongs exclusively to the Bishop, ordinary power is not invested in the Vicar Capitular or Administrator. For he performs such acts of jurisdiction only of which he is capable. Lastly, a new privilege is granted to the Vicar Capitular or Administrator which is a distinct departure from the old law,[23] for by it he can confer all those parochial offices, the appointment of which would otherwise belong to the Bishop, provided the See has been vacant for at least a year. He no longer needs to apply to the Holy See for this permission, as the law itself grants it.[24] In conformity with the corollary mentioned above, viz., that no one can confer a benefice on himself, it must be stated here, that an Administrator, during the vacancy of a See, cannot appoint himself to a benefice becoming vacant, even though he would probably be appointed to it, e. g., on account of his seniority, were the See not vacant.

In conclusion §3 of Canon 455 makes it very plain that the Vicar General enjoys none of the privileges of the Administrator unless he is administrating an impeded diocese. The Vicar

[21] Cf. cc. 184-195.
[22] Cf. cc. 429-430.
[23] Cf. c. 2, X, I, 9; cf. cc. 431-432.
[24] Cf. Wernz, Jus Decret., II, p. 969, not. 243.

General, as stated above, can never make an appointment to a parish unless he has a special mandate in writing to that effect. In only one case does the Vicar General not need such a special mandate and that is if the See is "Impedita" according to Canon 429 §1.

CHAPTER XIX

The Transfer of Pastors

To complete the question of appointment it is necessary to give a brief expose of the legislation in the Code regarding the transfers of pastors. A transfer is after all a sort of an appointment. By transfer is meant generally an exchange of parishes made with the consent of the legitimate superior. Some kind of reason at least is required for lawful transfers, because, as a rule, they are looked upon as odious unless they involve a promotion.[1]

The Code admits the welfare of souls (*bonum animarum*) as a valid reason. This is a restatement of the *"Maxima Cura"* principle, *"salus animarum, suprema lex."* The new legislation says that the competent superior may decree a transfer and draws a distinction between irremovable and movable pastors. On the other hand, even the old law, as well as the new, admitted that there is a difference between voluntary and involuntary transfers, or to a better or worse parish. It is worthy of note that the practice of the Roman Court concerns almost exclusively transfers of the so-called *"desservants"* of France, who were considered *"rectores ad nutum amovibiles."*

The Code states that if the welfare of souls requires that a pastor be transferred from a parish which he had governed with success to another parish, the Ordinary shall propose the matter to the pastor and persuade him to accept the transfer for the love of God and the good of souls. The reason for the transfer is here supposed to exist in the parish *to which* the pastor is to be transferred.[2] It may be that this parish is being financially or spiritually neglected, or that factions or parties are tearing it up to the detriment of souls.[3] The Ordinary, however, must

[1] Cf. Augustine, II, p. 167 ff.; A. S. S., XIX, 53 seqq.
[2] Cf. cc. 37, 39; c. 5, X, VIII, 19, mentions *"Utilitas et necessitas."*
[3] S. C. C., Mar. 27, 1886; A. S. S., XIX, 53.

duly consider the character of the pastor, whether he is movable or irremovable, and whether he is willing or not to accept the transfer, for the Ordinary has no right (*jure ordinario*) to transfer an *irremovable* pastor against his will to another parish. To do this special faculties from the Apostolic See are required. Whether the Ordinaries in the United States have obtained these special faculties cannot be stated with absolute certainty; at any rate, the formularies contain no such faculties.[4] The Ordinary should beware of making threats, because a transfer made under threat or by deceit, would be rescindable by the diocesan court.[5] Therefore, the Ordinary is not allowed to conceal the real condition of the parish *to which* an irremovable Pastor is to be transferred, though he may emphasize its advantages.

A removable Pastor may be transferred to another parish even against his will, provided the parish to which he is to be transferred is not of too low a rank, and provided the Ordinary *proceeds according to the canons of the Code.*

Just a word as to the meaning of the expression *"inferioris ordinis."* The inferiority may be owing to a smaller income, or to less importance, or to smaller size. The Pastor on his part may have his own ideas about the superiority or inferiority of a parish. If he accepts the parish offered to him, no further formality is required, except that he declare his willingness to accept, in order that the Ordinary may declare the parish vacant, but not by resignation, for it is a transfer, not a resignation. If the removable Pastor thinks he has reason for not accepting the new parish offered him, then: 1. He must in writing put the reasons for not accepting the transfer, e. g., his health, his mental qualities, his financial condition, etc.; 2. The Ordinary shall then consider the reasons carefully and weigh the status of a parish. If after due consideration he insists upon a transfer, he is bound, for valid procedure, to hear the opinions of two pastor-consultors on the reasons advanced, on the condition of both parishes (viz., the one from which and the one to which the removable Pastor is to be transferred), and finally, on the

[4] Not even the faculties (formula major III), granted lately to the vicars apostolic by the S. C. P. F. contained such faculty. Augustine mentioned the fact that he personally inspected the faculty of Right Reverend Leo Haid, O.S.B., formerly Vicar Apostolic of North Carolina, but he found no such permission given.

[5] Cf. c. 103; A. S. S. XI, 387.

reasons of necessity or utility which apparently demand a transfer. Here may be added some few remarks as to the attitude the Pastor in question should take while the case is pending. He should be careful to observe a discreet silence, and above all, not in any way to stir up or arouse the congregation or create factions, or what is still worse, have recourse to civil authority to bring pressure to bear on the Ordinary.[6] Such methods are not only unbecoming to a priest, but may exasperate the lawful authority and cause scandal. 2. After having heard the consultors, if the Ordinary still insists on the transfer, he may renew his paternal (*not canonical*) admonition to move the pastor to accept the change. 3. If this proves fruitless, and the Ordinary has made up his mind to abide by his former intention, he shall command the removable pastor (*Parocho Praecipiat*) to repair to the new parish within a certain time. This is a formal precept to be served in writing, wherein the Ordinary declares that, after the expiration of the time granted the pastor for going to his new parish, the parish which he holds at present will be *ipso facto* vacant. But a reasonable time should be given. Twenty-four hours is not considered reasonable.[7] Ten days is more acceptable.

After the expiration of the appointed time, if the removable pastor has not gone to the parish assigned him, his former parish must be declared vacant. Here the procedure ends. No recourse is mentioned. He can even be punished if he refuses to submit to the authority of the Ordinary.[8] The whole legislation is modern [9] and as stated, has grown out of the conditions of the past.

---

[6] S. C., Mar. 27, 1886; A. S. S. XI, 382, seqq.; XIX, 53 seqq.
[7] Cf. A. S. S. XI, 387
[8] Cf. Can. 2331, 2376.
[9] Cf. cc. 2157-2161; 2162-2167.

CHAPTER XX

THE TIME OF APPOINTMENT

Canon 458

Vacanti paroeciae curet loci Ordinarius providere ad normam Can. 155, nisi peculiaria locorum ac personarum adiuncta, prudenti Ordinarii iudicio, collationem tituli paroecialis differendam suadeant.

I. *Time of Appointment*

From the reading of this canon, it is readily understood that the Ordinary, unless peculiar circumstances of persons or places make a delay advisable, shall provide for a vacant parish in his diocese according to Canon 155. A parish becomes vacant *"de jure"* by the death, resignation (renunciation),[1] transfer, or deposition of the former pastor. A parish may be *"de jure"* vacant and at the same time *"de facto"* held unlawfully by an intruder.[*] In such a case the Ordinary should mention this fact in the letter of appointment of the new parish. If Canon 155 is applied

[1] The renunciation may be explicit or tacit. Tacit renunciation is as follows: Ob tacitam renuntiationem ab ipso iure admissam quaelibet officia vacant ipso facto et sine ulla declaratione, si clericus. 1°. Professionem religiosam emiserit, salvo, circa beneficia, praescripto Can., 584. 2°. Intra tempus utile iure statutum, vel, deficiente iure, ab Ordinario determinatum de officio provisus illud adire neglexerit. 3°. Aliud officium ecclesiasticum cum priore incompatibile acceptaverit et eiusdem pacificam possessionem obtinuerit. 4°. A fide Catholica publice defecerit. 5°. Matrimonium, etiam civile tantum, ut aiunt, contraxerit. 6°. Contra praescriptum Can., 141, 1 militiae saeculari nomen sponte dederit. 7°. Habitum ecclesiasticum propria auctoritate sine iusta causa deposuerit, nec illum, ab Ordinario monitus, intra mensem a monitione recepta resumpserit. 8°. Residentiam, qua tenetur, illegitime deseruerit et receptae Ordinarii monitioni, legitimo impedimento non detentus, intra congruum tempus ab Ordinario praefinitum, nec paruerit, nec responderit (Can., 188).

[*] Cf. Maroto, Institutiones Juris Canonici, p. 684, footnote (4).

here, the conclusion is that the appointment must be made within six months of the date on which the Ordinary becomes cognizant of the vacancy. When the Bishop delays the appointment, it should be for some reason, e. g., the moral or material circumstances of the place, for instance unpaid debts, unsafe conditions by reason of the fluctuating population, the erection of a parish school, the advisability of punishing the people for their treatment of a former pastor, etc. The circumstances of persons have reference to the person of the appointee, e. g., if there be a lack of priests qualified for the place, etc.

During the war, owing to the abnormal conditions, the Congregation of the Council sanctioned officially such delays.[2] After the war the permission was revoked. Should the vacancy be prolonged through the negligence of the Ordinary, beyond the allotted time, the appointment, according to the common law of the Church, would devolve upon the Holy See.[3]

The time limit of six months seems to be applicable only to those parishes which are of free collation. If the privilege of patronage is enjoyed, then the right of presentation should be claimed within four months,[4] or else the parish devolves upon the Ordinary of the place and becomes for that time, of free collation. Like presentation in the right of *"juspatronatus"* the right of election must be exercised according to first Article of Chapter I of Title IV in the second book of the Code. That means for election that if it is not made use of within three months, it is lost, and the Ordinary can then appoint whom he chooses.[5]

The confirmation of election has no time limit and can be protracted in many instances. Institution, however, ought to

---

[2] Cf. Nov., 14, 1916, A. A. S., VIII; Cocchi, p. 389; Ayrinhac, General Legislation in the Code, p. 324.

[3] Cf. Can. 1432, §3.

[4] If a bishop does not grant institution within the time prescribed for filling the vacancies and this through negligence, then the institution devolves upon the Metropolitan. Cf. Bened., XIV, "Cum Illud," §2.

[5] According to Canon 161, an electoral college has three months to fill a vacancy, unless ruled otherwise by special provision. The time is *"tempus utile,"* and as said above, it does not run when not usable. If the election is not made within the time prescribed, the electors lose their prerogative and the appointment to the office devolves upon the ecclesiastical superior or on the one whom the law empowers to supply the negligence or incapacity of the electoral college. Cf. Can., 432.

be granted within two months after the presentation has been made, unless there be a just impediment.[6]

The *tempus utile,* which is mentioned in Canon 155, begins from the moment that the Ordinary receives the notification of the vacancy and is reckoned according to the canon of *Titulus III De Temporis Supputatione.*[7] The law calls the requisite number of months *"Menses utiles,"* which implies that they do not run if the Superior is prevented from exercising his right.[8] In accordance with the prescription of Canon 34 §3, they should be taken as they stand in the calendar, not counting the first day.

Canon 159 says that appointments to ecclesiastical offices must be made in writing.

---

[6] Cf. Canon 1457.
[7] Cf. Canon, 31-36.
[8] Cf. Can., 35.

CHAPTER XXI

The Manner of Appointment

Canon 459

§1. Loci Ordinarius, graviter onerata eius conscientia obligatione tenetur vacantem paroeciam illi conferendi, quem magis idoneum ad eam regendam habuerit, sine ulla personarum acceptione.

§2. In hoc judicio ratio haberi debet non solum doctrinae, sed etiam earum omnium qualitatum, quae ad paroeciam vacantem rite regendam requiruntur.

§3. Quare loci Ordinarius:

> **1°. Ne omittat documenta, si qua sint, ex curiae tabulario desumere quae clericum nominandum respiciunt et notitias, secretas quoque, si opportunum judicaverit, prudenter exquirere etiam ex locis extra dioecesim;**
> **2°. Prae oculis habeat praescriptum Can. 130, §2;**
> **3°. Clericum examini super doctrina coram se et examinatoribus synodalibus subjiciat; a quo, de consensu eorundem examinatorum, potest dispensare, si agatur de sacerdote doctrinae theologicae laude commendato.**

§4. In regionibus in quibus paroeciarum provisio fit per concursum sive specialem ad normam const. Benedicti XIV Cum illud, 14 Dec. 1742, sive generalem, haec forms retineatur, donec Sedes Apostolica aliud decreverit.

From the whole tenor of this canon, it can be seen Holy Mother the Church wishes Bishops to be keenly alive to the necessity of providing suitable, nay rather the *most suitable* priests for the care of souls. This in very truth is a most weighty office since the eternal salvation of numerous souls is involved. How many souls may be saved or lost through the fruitful or barren ministry of the Priest? The Bishop then must take most seriously his duty in this respect and is bound in conscience to confer a vacant parish only on him whom he deems best fit for the office. He is strictly warned against the evil of being influenced in any way by favoritism and personal preferences. The grave obligation is hereby imposed upon all local Ordinaries to select for the pastoral office, among all the available candidates, the one best equipped for the government of the parish both spiritually and temporally. Motives extrinsic to the case should in no way influence his decision. The Code enacts that when an office becomes vacant by resignation or sentence of privation, the Superior who accepted the resignation or pronounced the sentence of privation cannot validly confer the office on his own relations by blood or marriage to the second degree inclusively nor on a member of his household. He cannot confer it either on the relations of the person who resigned it.[1]

By a vacant parish is meant one that has been newly erected or whose incumbent has died (total mental incapacity, or insanity is considered as an equivalent to physical death), or has been promoted to another parochial benefice, or who has been removed, or transferred or deposed,[2] or who resigned. A parish is considered as vacant (*de jure*) for any of the above mentioned causes.

There is somewhat of a discussion concerning the degree of fitness [3] required in the appointee. It can be held that the appointment of a less worthy in preference to a notably worthier

---

[1] Cf. Pius IV, *"Cupientes,"* October 11, 1560, Fontes, 99; Pius V, *"Quanta Ecclesiae,"* April 1, 1568, §5, Fontes, 127.

[2] Cf. Canon 150, Maroto, I, p. 701 seqq.

[3] Anent the word "Idoneum," fit, Augustine in his Commentary (II, p. 529), insists on fitness rather than worthiness. He recalls the decrees of the Council of Trent concerning the examination of candidates for vacant parishes, which laid special stress on the necessity of such examinations, at the same time permitting no appeal. A solitary exception was made in favor of those who were presented by those of Universities. Cf. sess. VII, c. 13; sess. XXIV, c. 18; sess. XXV, c. 9, all "de ref.," Pius V, "In conferendis," April 15, 1567; Richter, Trid., etc., p. 55, p. 778, seqq.; Pius V, and Clement XI, issued constitutions to the same effect and Innocent XI, condemned the opinion which asserted that the Tridentine decrees were intended only to exclude the unworthy candidate and not to give preference to the more worthy. Bened. XIV, "Cum Illud," Code, Rome, 1919, Docum IV, p. 807; Bouix, De Parocho, p. 339.

candidate, although illicit, is not however declared invalid.[4] Passing over a worthier candidate would *not* for that reason alone, as long as the appointee be really worthy, render the appointment *"ipso facto,"* null, nor even rescindible,[5] at least not as a general rule. From a comparison with the legislation in other cases such as concursus, it seems evident that the Ordinary must choose here the most worthy among the worthy.[6] Cocchi [7] says that if the Ordinary chooses one that is unfit, then reparation is to be made, by removing that one and appointing one who is fit. If an Ordinary chooses the least fit among the fit, then, according to many, reparation is to be made. From this it may be understood why §1 of the canon appeals most earnestly to the Ordinary (*"graviter onerata ejus conscientia"*) exhorting him to appoint the fittest candidate (*magis idoneum*). No matter how wide the latitude be that one gives to the meaning of the word *"fit,"* the Bishop, who knowingly appoints to a vacant parish one who is unworthy, commits undoubtedly a serious sin.[8]

That he may form an objective and safe judgment of a candidate's fitness, the law enjoins the Ordinary to seek as much information about him as he deems advisable. There are many sources of such information. The records of the junior clergy examinations, which he passed during the early years of his priesthood, will furnish some idea of his acquired knowledge and practical application of the ecclesiastical sciences.[9] In forming the estimate of a candidate's fitness, the Ordinary must take into account not only his learning, but also the other qualities required for the successful administration of the particular parish

---

[4] Cf. Cocchi, vol. II; if the difference between the two is small, it can be disregarded. Cf. Aryinhac, Const. of Church, p. 322, §264; Fanfani, p. 86; Blat, vol. II, p. 490, n. 507; Raia, p. 38; De Meester, p. 258 and 259, §813; Chelodi, p. 372, B. of 224; Prummer, p. 210, §155.

[5] Maroto, I, p. 701. Such an appointment has never been held invalid *"per se,"* so far; but in the case of Concursus it is rescindable. (Thus Maroto, l. c.) *"in casu . . . concursus rescindibilis, minime vero in aliis cusibus ut magis videtur."* Cf. Wernz, Jus Decretalium, II, n. 311.

[6] Cf. Cocchi, p. 391, l. c.; Maroto says: *"magis idoneus seu dignior aut dignissimus,"* p. 697, n. 590, cf. Can. 153, §2; Blat says that the prescription of choosing the more worthy does not bind when the appointing has been passed on by devolution to one other than the Ordinary.

[7] Vol. 2, p. 391.

[8] Cf. De Meester, II, p. 259, n. c.; Cocchi, cc. 391; cf. Can., 2391.

[9] Cf. Can., 130.

which happens to be vacant at the time. Those qualities comprise besides his age, the orders received, his honesty of life. The moral requisites should consist in acquired virtue, probity of life, piety, prudence, zeal for souls.[10]

The new legislation warns the Bishop prudently to investigate the character of the appointee. He must therefore take means to find out his moral worth, executive ability, and other qualifications which make for the true pastor of souls. To ascertain this the legislator directs the Ordinary not to fail to consult all the documents which the archives of the diocese may contain with reference to the candidate; his fidelity to duty, his success in the work previously entrusted to him, etc. He should ask, if in his good judgment it appears expedient, prudently and discreetly, for secret information even outside the diocese.

I. *Examinations*

The Code suggests that there be at this time a special examination on the candidate's intellectual ability in the presence of the Board of Examiners (Synodal, or Pro-Synodal, examiners). The matter of this examination and its method depend on the examiners themselves. *It should be passed by every secular priest who is to be appointed to a parish, whether removable or irremovable, unless the applicant has distinguished himself in theology.* Wherein the distinction consists is not precisely stated, and hence room is left for discussion. "A Doctor of Sacred Theology who has received his degree from a Catholic University no doubt enjoys that distinction. But as no academic degree is mentioned, it would not be against the spirit of the law if a professor in the Episcopal Seminary were accorded the privilege of exemption. The term Theology is generally taken to comprise dogmatic, moral, and pastoral Theology as well as Holy Scripture. In its present form Canon Law really forms an integral part of Theological training, and furthermore a degree in Canon Law can be obtained only after a post-graduate course. It would be difficult then to imagine a solid canonist without a thorough knowledge of Theology proper and Church History likewise. We may safely then include licentiates, doctors and

[10] Cf. cc. 232, §1; 331, §1, 4°; 434, §2; 367, §1; 404, §1; 423, 453, §2; 1589, etc.

professors of that noble science in the category of the "*doctrinae theologicae laude commendati.*" [11]

However, the Bishop cannot decide this point by himself, but needs the consent of the examiners. This consent may be given by each one individually or by vote.[12]

The Commission for the Authentic Interpretation of the Code, explaining the provision of exemption from the examination accorded to some by the Code, made the following declaration, November 24, 1920:* 1. A pastor who has already proven his fitness for pastoral office and held a parish, need not take the examination again to move to another parish (if the initiative for the change comes from the Bishop. But he should take it, if he himself has asked for the transfer unless the Ordinary and Synodal examiners dispense him, considering that the proof he formerly gave of his ability suffices for the present appointment.) 2. A pastor removed from his parish by the administrative process as prescribed in Canon 2154, need not undergo another examination, before receiving a new appointment. 3. Nor does the obligation exist for a pastor whom his Ordinary officially asked to resign his parish that he might transfer him to another. 4. If an ecclesiastic whom the Bishop thinks fit for a parish refuses to submit to the examination, as may occur when the parish offered him is not very desirable or important (and the case does not come under any of the rules permitting exemption), it must be referred to the Congregation of the Council. (This implies clearly that the Ordinary has no power or authority to dispense from the law of examination.) 5. The examination undergone before the reception of major orders [13] may serve as a test of fitness for the first appointment to a parish, but on two conditions, viz., that they were passed in the presence of the Ordinary himself, and the Synodal examiners, and that they bore on all the subjects that formed the matter of the examination for parishes. 6. The examinations which are prescribed for young priests (Canon 130)

---

[11] Augustine, Commentary, II, p. 530. He refers to Bened., XIV, De Syn., XIII, 9, 17.

[12] Canon, 105, 2°.

* Cf. A. A. S., 1920, XII, p. 573.

[13] Cf. Can., 996, §2 and §3.

do not dispense from the regular examinations for parishes, even though they be passed in the presence of the Bishop and the Synodal examiners. These declarations are so clear that they do not need further elucidation.

II. *Concursus* [14]

The fourth paragraph of this Canon 459 treats of the concursus which is two-fold, either special as described by Benedict XIV, or general, which differs from the special concursus. The difference between the special and general concursus is this; that the special concursus is the competitive examination in the form prescribed by law which is held upon the vacancy of a parish, and the general concursus is an examination held at stated times, the results of which are used for the appointment to future vacancies. The Second Plenary Council of Baltimore adopted the constitution *"Cum illud"* for all irremovable rectorships. The Code does not repeat the statement of the Council of Trent that the concursus obliges *under pain of nullity.*[15] It commands explicitly that the regulation of the concursus be retained wherever it has been in use until the Holy See itself makes other provisions. Therefore the concursus should still be enforced in this country. The new legislation in no way abrogates particular law on this point.[16] In a particular case for a particular parish the Ordinary may dispense from this concursus, by virtue of Canon 291, §2. On the other hand it might be said that what was particular law prior to 1918 has on the publication of the Code, been converted into common law for this country. The substance of the Papal legislation on the question of concursus,

[14] Chelodi thinks that because the Code does not impose the concursus universally, in course of time it may be dropped. Cf. Chelodi, Jus de Personis, p. 375, d.; cf. C. C., April 13, 1918; A. A. S., XI, 236.

[15] Cf. Chelodi, Jus de Personis, p. 375. *"In aliquibus regionibus (Gallia Belgio) nullus adhibebatur concursus, cum ex consuetudine tolerati alio modo episcopi de scientia et quabitatibus promovendorum se certiores redderent,"* in footnote (I). *Discrimen inter forman Trid. et novam formam* provisionis in eo est quod in *illa* episcopus cum examinatoribus, in *hac* solus episcopus de idoneitate (excepta scientia) judicat. In multis regionibus concursus generalis de doctrina et specialis de aliis qualitatibus a diuturno tempore fit, nunquam aut vix nunquam querelae vel recursus occurerunt.

[16] Acta et Decreta Conc. Balt., n. 36, seqq., n. 40, seqq., p. 25, seqq.; Smith, Elements, I, p. 416, seqq.; cf., also chapter XI of this dissertation.

together with the regulations of the Council of Baltimore, have been given in detail in chapters X and XI in this disquisition. It might be recalled, however, that the German Bishops had proposed an annual concursus, especially for the larger dioceses, to be discussed at the Vatican Council. It will be recollected that this proposal was never brought to the attention of the Fathers of that meeting. Like the general concursus it was suggested that this examination should turn chiefly about the learning of the candidates. The other qualities were to be considered at the time the parish became vacant. Those who had successfully passed the examination were considered fit for any parish, so far as doctrine was concerned.

Since the legislation of the Third Plenary of Baltimore on those points not revoked by the Code still holds good for this country, its regulations must be borne in mind.[17] There is one very wise provision that only those priests who have been laudably engaged in the sacred ministry for at least ten years can be admitted to the concursus. They must have during that time in the diocese given some proof for their ability to govern a parish both spiritually and temporally. If the concursus were a general concursus, then, after six years, those who had passed it and had not as yet received a parish, must undergo another examination if they wish to be appointed to an irremovable rectorship. It must be observed that the Council of Baltimore prescribed this concursus examination only for irremovable pastorates. The general concursus was embodied by the same Council in its decrees,[18] and since the Code mentions it also, it is not looked upon at present as abolished. This general concursus originally was intended, but for those dioceses whose size does not permit calling a special concursus, and also owing to other peculiar circumstances mentioned which render a general concursus and not a special concursus advisable.

In stressing the advantage and even the necessity of these examinations, far be it from the intention of the writer to leave the impression that the judgment of the fitness of the appointee depends upon their result alone. The concursus surely has many good points in its favor, for without it, how could a Bishop appreciate at their full worth all of the members of the diocesan

[17] Cf. Can. 459, §4.

[18] III Plenary Council of Baltimore, Acta et Decreta, p. 30, §50, §59.

clergy? He must be careful in seeking information about any particular priest to avoid all sources that may be tainted by personal feeling. In large dioceses, such as many in the United States, the Bishop may find it difficult to have a continual close contact with all his priests. Moreover the fact that a parish may be financially successful, or numerically large, is no criterion of the efficiency of the pastor. Then, too, at times one man may reap the harvest of another man's labors. Popularity or even personality prove of little lasting use, though if they are properly directed, they may produce abundant fruit in the harvest of souls. Efficiency in this divine work is not for the day, but must last permanently. Therefore the Bishop must be very discerning and exercise great acumen in his judgment and valuation of the priests committeed to his care, and of the people as well. All the priests are not suited for every parish, nor are some suited for some parishes; let the Bishop then choose to the best of his discretion the right man for the right place.

One final question is: Can a Bishop confer a parish on a priest who is unwilling? According to Canon 128, a cleric must accept the office given him, unless he is prevented by a legitimate obstacle. Moreover, the first law given by the Code on benefices is Canon 1436, which says that a benefice cannot be validly conferred on an unwilling cleric, nor a cleric not expressly accepting the appointment. This is simply the repetition of a law found in the Corpus Juris Canonici.[19] Golden says: "In the United States the clergy are ordained under the title either of mission work, or of the service of the Church, and therefore should accept any charge given them by their Bishop."[20] If they be unreasonably unwilling, they may be punished by the Bishop.[21]

---

[19] C. 17, III, 4 in VI°.

[20] Cf. Golden: Parochial Benefices, p. 48.

[21] Can., 2331, 2376.

CHAPTER XXII

Unity and Institution

Canon 460

§1. Parochus ad normam Canon 156, unam tantum titulo paroeciam habeat, nisi de paroeciis agatur aeque principaliter unitis.

§2. In eadem paroecia unus tantum debet esse parochus qui actualem animarum curam gerat, reprobata contraria Consuetudine et revocato quolibet contrario privilegio.

Canon 461

Curam animarum parochus obtinet a momento captae possessionis ad normam Can. 1443-1445; et ante possessionem aut in ipso possessionis capiendae actu fidei professionem edere debet, de qua in Can. 1406, §1, 7°.

I. *Unity*

A parish priest, according to §1 of Canon 460, can hold only one parish "in titulum," unless two parishes are united "aeque principaliter."[1] In each parish only one priest is the parish priest, who has the actual care of souls; all contrary customs and privileges are repealed.[2] Hence Canon 460 speaks of the

[1] One only proper pastor is to be in charge of each parish. This law would be violated if several parishes were conferred *"in titulum"* on the same priest. This conferring would be invalid, as the offices are incompatible. (Can. 156) unless they are *aeque principaliter unita."*

[2] Cf. Chelodi—Jus De Personis, p. 372. It is a fact that in Italy some parishes are held by more than one pastor. There were canonists who claimed this was not against canon law; cf. Bouix, De Parocho, 188 seqq.; Hinschius, II, 395; the Cong. of the Council at times tolerated this condition, but prescribed certain conditions, and at the same time insisted that this state of affairs be abolished. It is evident that it is contrary to modern law, and modern parish organization.

incompatibility of two parish charges in one and the same person, and refers to the earlier legislation in the Code,[3] which forbids the holding of two offices that cannot be discharged at the same time by the same person. This law is taken from the Decretals[4] and the Council of Trent[5] and is partly based upon the requirement of residence, and partly upon the prohibition of avarice. The objection of incompatibility would not exist, if one of the offices was held only temporarily, as if a pastor had the administration of a second parish only for a time. Furthermore, benefices are held to be incompatible, when one suffices for the support of the holder.

A cleric loses *ipso facto* the office he holds if he accepts and obtains pacific or uncontested possession of another which is incompatible with the former.[6] If he attempts to retain the former also, he loses both. The Holy See may dispense from this law, but its intention of doing so must not be admitted without proof. The Pope would not confer an office upon a cleric who holds one that is incompatible with it, unless in asking for the second office the petitioner made mention of the one he already had; or, unless in the appointment, such derogatory clauses are used as manifest the intention of making an exception to the general rule. It must then be clear that the Holy See intends to confer on the same cleric two incompatible offices, or that it is willing to confer on him a certain office, even if he has already another regularly incompatible with it.

Hence one is not allowed to possess two parishes *"in titulum."* An exception is made in favor of two parishes united in such a way that they both retain their own titles and rights, and neither is subject to the other.[7] Note, however, that such a union must not be subjective, but objective, that is to say, the two parishes are not allowed to be united in favor of the pastor or holder, but purely with regard to themselves. For a subjective union would be nothing more than a veiled plurality of benefices, forbidden in the case of two parishes.

But what of two pastors who claim to have been appointed

---

[3] Canon 156.
[4] Cf. cc. 15, 18, X, III, 5, de praebend.
[5] Sess. VII, c. 13; sess. XXIV, c. 17, de ref.
[6] Cf. Can. 188.
[7] Cf. Can. 1419.

to the same parish? This can be settled by consulting the rescripts of appointment. The first prevails, provided they were both issued by the same Ordinary. If this should happen, and both rescripts dated the same day, they would both be invalid, unless one mentioned and revoked the other. The fact that the one with a prior claim should defer to the one with the less claim would not give the latter a legal right, unless there was a rescript stating this fact.[8]

The law of Canon 460, §2, would be transgressed, if in one and the same parish, several pastors, one independent of the other, exercised cumulatively jurisdiction over the same subjects. (Chelodi says of such a case: ". . . *quod monstrum sane dicendum est et prorsus interdicitur,*" "*reprobata contraria consuetudine et revocato quolibet contrario privilegio*" (Can. 460). This law governs not only parishes erected after the promulgation of the Code, but also those erected before 1918, though in them, the plurality of pastors was due not to custom or privilege but to legitimate statute.[9]

The second part of the canon safeguards the unity of government.[10] This is "directed against the interference on the part of the moral person. Sometimes there has been interference in such cases from the juridical person; (chapter or monastery, etc.); with the right of the pastor in the care of souls, it is likewise aimed at the encroachment on the part of assistants."[11] Needless to say, under the old law as under the new, several priests may be employed in the same parish, if one of them is designated as the pastor.

In some places the custom has existed to the present day of appointing to the same parish several pastors,[12] who exercise

[8] Cf. Can. 48-50.

[9] Cf. Can. I, July 14, 1922; A. A. S. XIV, 527; pro applicatione vero canonis ad casus particulares quoad jura parochis, ut aiunt, *proportionariis* seu cumulativis jam quaesita, tum quoad spiritualia tum quoad temporalia, recurrendum est ad C. C. item pro solutione quaestionis, utrum cura animarum principalis et unica tribuenda sit parocho qui praeeminentiam honoris habeat prae aliis, an vero antiquiori possessione; cf. Chelodi, Jus de Personis, p. 371; cf. Rossi, De Paroecia, pp. 82, 83.

[10] Cf. c. 41, c. 7, qu. 1, c. 4, c. 21, Qu. 2; where the allegory of husband and wife is alleged; c. 15, X, III, 4; Barbosa, De Parochi. I, 1, n. 43; Bouix, p. 190 ff.

[11] Cf. Augustine, Commentary, II, p. 535.

[12] The law is not so absolute as to forbid that the same church be the seat of two parishes where necessity demands it. Cf. Chelodi, Jus de Personis, p. 372.

authority in turn, or who divide it among them. The Code reprobates such a custom, and demands its suppression. But this does not refer to a condition that obtains in many of our American dioceses, especially in the larger cities, viz., that the same territory may be in two parishes, in this way that the limits of a national parish overlap those of several other diocesan city parishes. For after all the national pastor and the native pastor are not exercising their ministry over the same souls. The ministrations of the national pastors are to be restricted to the nationals. The rule of the canon is this: There cannot be two pastors for the same territorial parish.[13]

II. *Installation*

Canon 461 explains that the pastor has the care of souls from the moment of taking possession of the parish. Either before or during the act of taking possession, he must pronounce the profession of faith, and the oath against modernism.[14] The mere appointment itself (*verbal institution*), while it gives the right to the parish does not of itself confer the care of souls and the enjoyment of the rights of pastor until the appointee has taken possession according to the Canons 1443-1445.[15] For bishops there is always an installation, formally observed, before he obtains possession of his diocese.[16] Why then is there none for the pastor, who after all is to administer directly and immediately to the spiritual needs of the flock confided to him?

In this country there seems to be a great disregard for the mind of the Code on this point. At times not even the requirements for the appointment itself are observed. Appointment is a general term, and is applied to offices of free collation, or to the institution of a candidate legitimately presented or nominated, or to the confirmation of one elected or postulated (Canons 147-148). Now *appointments should be made in writing*.[17] To give only an oral appointment is certainly not in keeping with the legislation of the Church. Still less, is a notice

---

[13] Cf. Prümmer, Manuale, p. 207, n. 152.
[14] Cf. Canon 1406, §1, 7°.
[15] Canon 1472.
[16] Canons 332-334.
[17] Canon 159.

inserted in a newspaper, even though it be the official diocesan organ, if the appointee is not at the same time notified by personal letter. There should be a regular form of appointment.

The law states that for the actual taking possession of a parish, Canons 1443-1445 must be observed.[18] Now what are the consequences of this act of taking possession. If a pastor has not the legitimate possession of a parish, he cannot lawfully perform the function of the office, i. e., solemn baptism, administration of Viaticum, of Extreme Unction. Furthermore there arises a question of the validity of other acts, for instance, hearing confessions, if he has no faculties except those derived from his office; assistance at marriage according to Canons 1094, 1095, §1, 1°. Of course one realizes that Canon 209 supplies jurisdiction.

No one, *not even an appointee,* can take possession of a parish of his own power.[19] Installation must be granted by the Ordinary of the place, or through some other ecclesiastical person duly delegated by him (Canon 1443, §2). For this act the Code in the aforesaid canon uses the words, *"missio in possessionem,"* or *"institutio corporalis,"* and if we take it in conjunction with Canon 461 as the Code demands, then it must be understood as being an integral part of the appointment. The Code does not specify how this *"missio in possessionem"* for the pastor should take place as it does for the Bishop.[20] Canon 1444, §1, states that it should be carried out after the manner established by statute or by legitimate custom. The Synods of *certain dioceses* have drawn up a form to be followed, which though somewhat elaborate, yet inducts into office in a very significant way. Thus there is the giving of the keys to the Church with which the doors are locked and unlocked, the giving of the tabernacle key, etc.[21] Surely, aside from Canon Law at all, this is in keeping with the induction into offices as practiced in all lay organizations. Such a ceremony, because of the public character, could not but dignify the position of the pastor.

But what of the dioceses in the United States? Is it justifiable

---

[18] Cf. Fanfani, De Jure Parochorum, §96 b), §99 a), b); Rossi, De Paroecia, n. 180.

[19] Canon 1437.

[20] Canons 332-334.

[21] Cf. Rossi, De Paroecia, n. 182.

to disregard this point of legislation? It is not so much a question of what was done in the past, as what should be done in the future. Before 1908, it was never decided that all our parishes were canonical parishes or benefices. In the mission state of this country much could have been tolerated that is not legitimate now. But as far as is known to the writer, no steps have been taken anywhere in this country to introduce such a ceremony. Granted that the Ordinary can in writing dispense from the form in an individual instance, he cannot dispense from the act altogether. The time has come to prescribe a set form as indicated in Canon 1444, §1.

Can one support the present practice on the ground that it is an immemorial custom? But what of the effect of Canon 5 on those customs that are found even in unwritten law? And of Canon 6, for the particular legislation in written law? What was lawful because of custom, when the parishes in this country were not declared canonical parishes and benefices, cannot for that reason be considered lawful after such a declaration.[22] On the other hand after only eleven years under the new legislation, we cannot claim a legitimately prescribed custom.[23] The dispensation that the Ordinary may grant according to Canon 1444, §1, is not from any installation whatsoever, but from the observance of the form prescribed by statute or legitimate custom. Custom cannot, then, be invoked in this case.

The writer holds for the observance of some form of installation, besides the statement that Father N. N. will take up his duties as pastor of St. N.'s Church, beginning on such a date. The reasons are as follows: First, the matter of liceity and validity of the acts already mentioned. When there is a question of the validity of an act, caution must be taken. Secondly, as has already been said, no one can take possession of an office by his own power. Thirdly, the Code distinguishes between the *appointment* and the *taking possession*. Fourthly, though Canon 209 (*propter errorem communem*) supplies the validity for many acts, yet if, as the Code states in Canon 461, the care of souls begins with the *"missio in possessionem"* (*a momento captae*

---

[22] Cf. S. C. Cons. Declaratio, Aug. 1, 1919, A. A. S., XI (1919), 346-7; letter of Apostolic Delegate, Nov. 10, 1922.

[23] Canon 28.

possessionis), then the *"missio in possessionem"* is as necessary as the letter or decree of appointment.

In our country a practice not at all in conformity with Canon 1444, §1, seems to be followed, viz., that in the absence of a prescribed form of *corporal institution* the appointee proceeds as the local Ordinary instructs, and probably *legitimately* takes possession of the parish.[24] His possession starts from the moment within the time specified by the Ordinary, that he enters upon the parish. Of course, one does not expect the Ordinary personally to install all pastors of his diocese. He can very easily delegate some other priest to do so. For country parishes, he could give a general delegation to the rural deans, that they might carry out all the installations in their deaneries, etc.

If a pastor does not wish to be present himself at the function of installation, he may be represented by a procurator endowed with a special mandate. If the appointee fails to take charge of the parish within the time specified by the local Ordinary, unless hindered by a lawful obstacle, the parish should be declared vacant. The neglect of the appointee is interpreted as a tacit renunciation of the parish according to Canon 188, 2°.

III. *Institution*

The act of granting installation to one elected, or presented or nominated to a parish is called institution. Institution consists chiefly in the approval of such a candidate by the local Ordinary. This approval by the Ordinary is so necessary that if one should take possession of the parish, or interfere in its administration without it, he makes himself liable to the penalties of Canon 2394.[25] The religious presented by the religious superior to the Ordinary, and approved by him does not need the corporal institution as prescribed for the secular priest,[26] who becomes *"parochus."* In this country the religious are the only ones who enjoy the right of presentation since neither the right of patronage nor election have ever been granted here.

[24] Cf. Reg. 1, R. J. in VI°; Reg. 68, 72, R. J. in VI°; Compare Canon 2394.

[25] The penalties inflicted by Canon 2394 are incurred also by an intruder, i. e., one who has not even a *jus ad rem* as is enjoyed by those elected, presented or nominated to a benefice. Cf. Chelodi, Jus Poenale, n. 105.

[26] Cf. Fanfani, De Jure Parochorum, n. 96 A), 99 B).

IV. *The Profession of Faith*

The Council of Trent required pastors to make a profession of faith at least within two months after taking possession of their benefice, under penalty of losing the fruits thereof.[27] The present law *demands* that this profession of faith *be made* before the installation or as a part of the ceremony of installation, and *Canon 2403 directs the Ordinary to give warning to those who neglect to do so, and to punish them even with privation of their office if they do not comply with the law within the time specified.*

The profession of faith is made in the hands of the Bishop or his delegate and according to the form given at the beginning of Cardinal Gasparri's edition of the Code, and often designated as the *"Professio Piana."* To the profession of Faith, Pius X, of blessed memory, in the Const. "Sacrorum Anstitutum,"[28] prescribed the addition of the anti-modernist oath, and the Holy Office demanded, March 22, 1918, that this rule remain in force after the promulgation of the Code, until the Holy See abrogates it. The profession of faith cannot validly be made by proxy. *The Code explicitly and specifically condemns all customs contrary to the legislation on the profession of the faith.*[29]

---

[27] Sess. XXIV, c. 12 de ref.

[28] Sept. 1, 1910; A. A. S. II (1910), 669; S. C. S. Off. March 22, 1918, A. A. S. X (1918), 136.

[29] C. 1408.

APPENDIX

Formula erectionis novae paroeciae per creationem[1]

N. Episcopus N.

Cum in visitatione nuper per Nos facta invenerimus in loco N. non adesse ecclesiam parochialem, in qua Christi fideles ibidem commorantes sacramenta recipere et monita salutis audire possint . . .: propterea gregis nobis commissi consulere, et malis quae ex pastoris deficientia occurrere in dies solent providere volentes, attenta praesertim hominum dicti loci humili instantia et supplicatione pro erectione parochialis ecclesiae, ac obligatione per eosdem solvendi certam pecuniarum summam parocho pro tempore eligendo, ut commode sustentari possit, (donec de congrua sustentatione aliunde provideatur): invocato Domini Nostri Iesu Christi Nomine, eiusque Matris semper Virginis Mariae, ecclesiam loci N. sub invocatione Sancti N. huius nostrae dioecesis, nostra auctoritate ordinaria et omni, etc., tenore praesentium in parochialem cum suo territorio et districtu a loco . . . ad locum . . . erigimus et erectam volumus et declaramus: ecclesiaeque praedictae sic in parochialem erectae iura omnia et privilegia quae parochialibus de iure competunt concedimus et illis gaudere debere decernimus, cum assignationibus et proventibus a praefatis parochianis promissis ac aliis obvenientibus eleemosynis, et obligationibus universis, certis et incertis, a sacris canonibus concessis et permissis. Ipsamque ecclesiam paroecialem (nulli iuris patronatus servituti subiectam esse, sed) ad liberam nostram et successorum nostrorum collationem et provisionem, servata forma a sacris canonibus praescripta, spectare et pertinere decernimus. Ut autem praefata ecclesia parochialis noviter erecta de idoneo rectore provideatur qui populo in divinis et animarum cura regenda prosit, et Missas diebus festivis pro ovibus suis celebrare, Sacramenta ministrare aliaque parochialia munia implere debeat et teneatur, dilectum

[1] These first four *Formulae* are taken from Fanfani, De Jure Parochorum, pp. 399-407.

Nobis in Christo Dom. N. presbyterum, per Nos et examinatores nostros synodales tanquam habilem et idoneum repertum praeficimus, illique curam, regimen et administrationem Sacramentorum committimus, ac eidem de praefata ecclesia parochiali de novo erecta collationem facimus et providemus. Mandantes, etc. In quorum, etc.

Datum —. N. EPISCOPUS N.

N. Cancellarius Episcopalis.

Formula erectionis novae Paroeciae per dismembrationem seu divisionem

N. EPISCOPUS N.:

Ea quae animarum pericula submovent et populo Nobis credito levamina praebent sedulo amplectentes, supplicationibus fidelium loci N. inclinati, quibus dolentes Nobis exposuerunt, quod cum ipsi sub paroecia sancti N. loci N. exsistant, ob distantiam (vel aliam legitimam causam, e. gr. ob impedimentum fluminis N., quod paroeciam dividit et rapide decurrit, praesertim tempore hiemali, nec non asperam coenosamque viam, etc.), non possint, praesertim senes, pueri ac debiles, absque maxima difficultate et periculo, ad illam pro divinis officiis audiendis et percipiendis Sacramentis accedere: quodque persaepe sine illis quamplures ex hac vita discesserint; neque sufficienter provisum sperare fas sit per alium sacerdotem qui in capella seu ecclesia Sancti N. Missam diebus festis celebret et Sacramenta in casu necessitatis ministret: ad dismembrationem et erectionem respective novae paroeciae, prout ipsi postularunt, procedere statuimus.

Idcirco, facta per vicarium nostrum generalem, de mandato nostro, diligenti super expositis inquisitione; citato etiam et audito domino Rmo. Parocho ecclesiae paroecialis N.: dictum locum N. cum ecclesia Sancti N. hominibus, incolis et familiis a parochiali ecclesia loci N. auctoritate ordinaria a Codice I. C. (can. 1427, §1) nobis concessa, separamus, dividimus et dismembramus, et dictam ecclesiam Sancti N., cum suo loco et districtu a loco . . . usque ad locum . . . in parochialem ecclesiam erigimus et constituimus: dantes et concedentes incolis et habitatoribus dicti loci et districtus plenam et liberam potestatem, in dicta parochiali ecclesiis sepulturas, coemeterium, fontem baptismalem, campanile, campasas et alia insignia parochialitatis constituendi et retinendi.

Pro exercitio autem curae in populum et utriusque sexus fideles in dicto loco et districtu habitantes, dilectum Nobis in Christo presbyterum N., qui populo et ecclesiac praedictis in divinis et animarum cura regenda praesit, tanquam habilem, idoneum ab examinatoribus synodalibus examinatum et approbatum, praeficimus et deputamus, illique administrationem omnium sacramentorum ecclesiae committimus, et de ecclesia parochiali sic noviter erecta providemus . . . (Si nova paroecia dotetur ex reditibus ecclesiae a qua dividitur, additur):

Volentes et mandantes rectori dictae ecclesiae Sancti N. matricis, et aliis pro tempore exsistentibus, quatenus de cetero singulis annis, tempore . . . dicto Dom. N. et suis in dicta ecclesia parochiali per Nos noviter erecta curatis successoribus de reditibus suae ecclesiae persolvat. . . . Ut autem ad tramitem can. 1427 §4, dictae ecclesiae matrici debitus honor servetur et exhibeatur, volumus . . . (et determinatur hic modus, quomodo huiusmodi honor sit exhibendus: e. gr. ut offeratur libram cerae, etc.).

Itaque auctoritate nostra quae supra dismembramus, erigimus, assignamus et reservamus, omni, etc.

Datum —.

N. Episcopus N.,
N. Cancellarius Episcopalis.

Formula collationis ecclesiae parochialis per concursum

N. Episcopus N.:

Dilecto nobis in Christo presbytero N., salutem in Domino.— Inter cetera, quae pro pastoralis officii debito praestare cupimus, illud praecipue cordi est, ut parochialibus ecclesiis, quibus de rectoribus providendum est, tales praeficiamus, qui ministerio curae animarum, quod omnium gravissimum est, laudabiliter satisfaciant. Vacante igitur a die . . . parochiali ecclesia sub invocatione Sancti N. loci N. huius nostrae Dioecesis per obitum (vel renuntiationem) N. illus. dum diveret, ultimi possessoris, fuerunt per curiam nostram, mediante publico edicto iuxta formam et praescriptum sacrorum canonum, vocati omnes de sic vacante ecclesia providere cupientes, quatenus intra terminum quindecim (vel. . . .) dierum comparerent in eadem curia ad faciendum describi et adnotari nomina ipsorum: et cum in eodem termino plures comparuissent, tandem iisdem legitime vocatis sub die . . . coram Nobis, rigoroso praevio examine per examinatores synodales facta fuit experientia de scientia et sufficientia singulorum descriptorum; ac demum servatis de iure servandis, per dictos examinatores tanquam magis idoneus vita et moribus, aetate et scientia et aliis a iure requisitis reputatus et iudicatus fuisti. Nos igitur eidem ecclesiae, ac animabus illi subditis de rectore providere volentes, tibi quem prae ceteris digniorem delegimus, eamdem parochialem, cum illis adnexis ac omnibus iuribus et pertinentiis suis universis, conferimus et assignimus, de illaque te investimus. Quocirca mandamus ut intra spatium . . . a praesenti die . . . computandum praedictae ecclesiae parochialis ac omninum annexorum et pertinentium secundum modum legitima consuetudine in dioecesi nostra receptum et praemissa professione Fidei, per teipsum vel per procuratorem possessionem accipias (can. 461), amoto exinde quolibet illicito detentore, quem Nos harum serie amovemus et denuntiamus amotum.

(*Si autem contingat eum, cui de beneficio providetur, aliud incompatibile iam obtinere, tunc additur:* Volumus autem ac praesentium tenore declaramus, per huiusmodi parochialis pacificam possessionem, alteram parochialem ecclesiam N. (vel praebendam canonicalem) quam obtines, eo ipso vacare).

In quorum, etc.

Datum —.

N. Episcopus N..

N. Cancellarius Episcopalis.

Formula collationis ecclesiae parochialis per Liberam Collationem

N. Episcopus N.:

Dilecto nobis in Christo presbytero N., salutem in Domino.— Inter cetera, quae pro pastoralis officii debito praestare cupimus, illud praecipue cordi est, ut parochialibus ecclesiis, quibus de rectoribus providendum est, tales praeficiamus, qui ministerio curae animarum, quod omnium gravissimum est, laudabiliter satisfaciant. Vacante igitur a die . . . parochiali ecclesia sub invocatione Sancti N. loci N. huius nostrae Dioecesis per obitum (vel renuntiationem) N. illus, dum viveret, ultimi possessoris. Nos igitur eidem ecclesiae, ac animabus illi subditis de rectore providere volentes, tibi, quem prae ceteris digniorem delegimus, eamdem parochialem, cum illis adnexis ac omnibus iuribus et pertinentiis suis universis, conferimus et assignamus, de illaque te investimus. Quocirca mandamus ut intra spatium . . . a praesenti die . . . computandum praedictae ecclesiae parochialis ac omnium annexorum et pertinentium secundum modum legitima consuetudine in dioecesi nostra receptum et praemissa professione Fidei, per teipsum vel per procuratorem possessionem accipias (can. 461), amoto exinde quolibet illicito detentore, quem Nos harum serie amovemus et denuntiamus amotum. (Si autem contingat eum, cui de beneficio providetur, aliud incompatibile iam obtinere, tunc additur: Volumus autem ac praesentium tenore declaramus, per huiusmodi parochialis pacificam possessionem, alteram parochialem ecclesiam N. (vel praebendam canonicalem) quam obtines, eo ipso vacare).

In quorem, etc.

Datum —. N. Episcopus N.,
N. Cancellarius Episcopalis.

Formula for Appointment of a Movable Pastor.[1]

N. Bishop of N., to our beloved, etc., Greeting:

Since the church of St. N. in the city (town) of N. in our diocese has become vacant by the death (resignation, transfer, promotion) of the Rev. N. N. its former pastor, and since for the good of souls it is necessary that we provide a pastor for the said church, who shall be . . . movable *ad normam juris;* we therefore, having confidence in your knowledge, piety, prudence, experience and general character, do by these presents appoint you to the said vacant church with its care of souls, . . . granting you all and singular the necessary rights and powers as movable rector of the said church in accordance with the Code and our diocesan statutes. Further we commend all whom it may concern to recognize you as such pastor and rector and give you all necessary assistance. In testimony whereof, etc.

Given, etc.

[L. S.] N. Bishop of N.,
N. N. Chancellor of Bishop.

[1] Cf. Baart, Legal Formulary, p. 110, n. 110.

A Tentative Right of Installation.[1]

1. The clergy vested in cassock and surplice meet in the Sacristy and assemble for the procession. In front of them will walk the members of the various parish societies. The procession will be led by the Cross-Bearer and Acolytes and will proceed first to the rectory. The Bishop or his Delegate (the Delegate of the Bishop for rural Parishes is usually the rural Dean, or if the rural Dean is the new Pastor the Delegate is the neighboring rural Dean; and in the city it is usually the senior Pastor or in his absence the Pastor next in seniority) will vest in his proper robes, and the administrator of the Parish will wear a stole as well as a surplice; the new Pastor will be vested only in cassock and surplice or if he be a Monsignor in his proper robes. The Bishop (or his Delegate), the administrator of the parish and the new Pastor who will be waiting in the rectory, join the procession there.

2. The procession proceeds to the church in this order, first, the Cross-Bearer and Acolytes; second, the parish societies; third, the clergy; and last the Bishop or his Delegate with the new Pastor at his left. The *Benedictus* is sung during the procession.

3. When the procession arrives at the door of the church the clergy separate in order to allow the Bishop or his Delegate with the new Pastor to take their places on the chairs placed before a table which should be prepared in the vestibule of the church. (If the Bishop is not present, his Delegate will ask one of the other priests to read aloud the act of delegation. Two other priests will stand on either side of the reader to act as witnesses.)

4. Next the procession proceeds up the center aisle of the church and after the usual genuflections the parish societies will take their places in the pews and the clergy will proceed to the sanctuary. They will genuflect and go to the kneeling benches. After the new Pastor has made his genuflection, the administrator will give him a crucifix to kiss. The *Veni Creator* is intoned, after which the *Oration* is sung by the Bishop (or his Delegate). Then the Bishop (or the Delegate) will go up to

---

[1] This is a translation from the Italian, Rite of Installation, used in diocese of Bergamo. Cf. It was drawn up by the Synod of 1910. Rossi, De Paroecia, n. 182.

the predella of the altar and stand at the Epistle side; the new Pastor with the administrator at his left, will stand on the first step of the altar in front of the Bishop (or his Delegate). The Bishop (or his Delegate) takes the stole from the administrator and puts it on the new Pastor.

5. The Bishop (or his Delegate) then conducts the new Pastor to his kneeling bench and motions him to sit down, saying to him: *"Ad multos annos hic sede veluti dux et rector hujus populi."*

6. He will then conduct him to the main altar where the new Pastor kisses the table of the altar first in the center and then at the sides. The Bishop (or his Delegate) now gives him the key of the tabernacle which he opens as these words are said: *"Haec est porta paradisi; aperi illam dignis, et ne des sanctum canibus, ut inveniaris fidelis dispensator mysteriorum Dei."*

7. He next conducts him to touch the sacred vessels placed on the Credence table, saying to him: *"Haec vasa divinis mysteriis destinate, semper te custodiente, munda sint, et populus cognoscat te diligere decorem Domus Dei."*

8. Then he will give him the oil stocks to touch as he says: *"Sicut infantes salutari lavacro abluendo per Uunctionem Sacram dispones; ita fideles ex hac vita profiscientes Oleo salutis inunge, et si in peccatis sint, remittantur eis."*

9. Then the Bishop (or his Delegate), the new Pastor and an altar boy carrying a bell, and the holy water stoop with the sprinkler, proceed to the Baptistry which is open. As they enter the Bishop (or his Delegate) says: *"Accede ad fontem aquae vivae, suscipe custodiam ejus, ut natos saeculo possis baptismate regenerare Deo."*

10. From here they advance to the confessional, a motion being made to the new Pastor to take his seat there as these words are addressed to him: *"Facies judicium rectum, ut remittas peccata, et dones gratiam per merita Christi Jesu."*

11. On leaving the confessional they will go to the vestibule of the church, here the new Pastor rings the bell softly as these words are said to him: *"Ad te spectabit imperare sonitum, quo audito, populus tuus ingredi concupiscat atria Domini."*

12. Next the new Pastor opens and closes the door of the church, turning the key in the lock as these words are pronounced: *"Accipe claves ecclesiae ad cutodiendum atria Domini,*

et dilige decorem domus ejus, tanquam sponsam ornatam viro suo."

13. After this as they turn back to advance again up the main aisle towards the altar, the Bishop (or his Delegate) gives the sprinkler to the new Pastor saying: *"Benedic populum istum, serva et custodi illum, et dirige eum in viam salutis aeternae."*

The new Pastor will bless the people as he advances, at the same time he recites in a low voice: *"Asperges me Domine."*

14. Finally he will go into the pulpit or on a platform (if there be no pulpit), and then the Bishop or his Delegate will present the new Pastor to the people with a few brief remarks. The new Pastor will then give a short sermon, after which if it is in the morning (this is the most desirable time), he will then sing the mass. After mass the *"Te Deum"* is intoned.

15. After the ceremony, the Priest who read the act of delegation will read from the sanctuary the formula for the act of giving possession. Now this document should be signed by the Bishop (or his Delegate), the new Pastor, the Administrator, and two witnesses from among the clergy. This document [1] should be forwarded to the Chancery Office.

---

[1] Formula of the Act: In nomine Domini. Amen. Under the Roman Pontificate of His Holiness (name and number) Pope, Right Rev. (or Most Rev.) N. N. being Bishop (or Archbishop) of the Diocese of ...., at this date............, I, Rev. .... (As delegate of the diocesan Ordinary), give to Rev. .... the canonical possession of the parish of .... to which he has been canonically appointed, in the presence of the under-signed .... who has acted as administrator during the vacancy, and the two witnesses, ... The Rev.................. is now canonically installed in the possession of this parochial benefice, as this act of date................ testifies. (The act of delegation was read, and) the act of possession publicly proclaimed.

Given this day .... of the month............... of the year........

(Signed) The Bishop (or Delegate), *The New Pastor.*

(The administrator during vacancy)

First witness: Second witness:

BIBLIOGRAPHY

JURIDICAL SOURCES

Acta Apostolicae Sedis, Romae, 1909.

Acta Sanctae Sedis, 41 vols., Romae, 1869-1908.

Acta et Decreta Conciliorum Recentiorum, Collectio, Lacensis, 7 vols., Friburgi Brisg., 1870.

Bullariun Romanum, 24 vols., Augustae Taurinorum, 1857-1872.

Canones et Decreta Concilii Tridentini, Taurini, 1913.

Codex Juris Canonici, Romae, 1917-1919.

Codex Theodosianus.

Codicis Juris Canonici Fontes, Cura Petri Card. Gasparii Editi, vols. I-IV, Romae, 1923-1926.

Collectanea S. Congregationis de Prop. Fide, 2 vols., Romae, 1907.

Corpus Juris Canonici, ed. Lipsiensis Secunda, Richter-Friedberg, 2 vols., Lipsiae, 1922.

Corpus Juris Civilis, ed. Mommseu Krueger, Berolini, 1915.

Decreta Concilii Plenarii Baltimorensis II, Baltimore, 1867.

Decreta Concilii Plenarii Baltimorensis III, Baltimore, 1886.

Mansi, J. D., *Sacrorum Conciliorum Nova et Amplissima Collectio.*

Summa Apostolicarum Decisionum extra ius Commune Vagantium. Editio Ultima Aucta et Recognita, Romae, 1658.

Thesaurus Resolutionum S. C. Concilii, 167 vols., 1718-1908.

WORKS OF REFERENCE

Augustine, Chas., *A Commentary on the New Code of Canon Law, II* ed., St. Louis, 1923.

———, *The Canonical and Civil Status of Catholic Parishes in the United States,* St. Louis, 1926.

Aichner, Simon, *Compendium Juris Ecclesiastici,* 6 ed., Brixinae, 1887.

Ayrinhac, H. A., *Constitution of the Church in the New Code of Canon Law,* New York, 1925.

———, *General Legislation in the Code,* New York, 1923.

———, *Legislation on the Sacraments,* New York, 1928.

Baart, Peter J., *Legal Formulary,* 2 ed., New York, 1898.

Barbosa, Augustine, *De Officio et Potestate Parochi,* Romae 1774.

Bardenhewer, Otto, *Patrology, Translated from the Second Edition by T. J. Shahan,* St. Louis, 1908.

Bargilliat, M., *Praelectiones Juris Canonici,* 24 ed., 2 vols., Pariisis, 1907; 28 ed., 2 vols., Pariisis, 1913.

———, XXVII ed., Paris, 1923.

Battiffol, P., *La Paix Constantinienne et le Catholicisme,* Paris, 1914.

Benedict XIV, *De Synodo Diocesana,* Romae, 1806.

Billot, Ludovicus, *Tractatus de Ecclesia Christi,* 2 vols., Romae, 1897.

Blat, Alberto, *Commentarium Textus Codicis Juris Canonici, lib. 2 De Personis,* Romae, 1921.

Bohmerus, J., *Jus Parochiale,* Editio Quarta, Halae, 1703.

Boudinhon, A., *Inamovibilite et Translation Des Desservants, Extrait de "la Correspondance Catholique,"* Paris (N. D.).

Bouix, D., *Tractatus De Parocho,* 2 ed., Parisiis, 1867.

————, *Tractatus De Parocho,* 3 ed., Parisiis, 1880.

Canones et Decreta Concilii Tridentini, ed. Richter-Schulte, Lipsiae, 1853.

Carmignani, Clemente, *Il Piccolo Codice,* Arezzo, 1927.

Catholic Encyclopedia, 15 vols., New York, 1907-1912.

Chelodi, Joannes, *Jus De Personis,* Trent, 1927.

Claeys-Bouuaert, Ferd., *De Canonica Cleri Saecularis Obedientia,* Tomus Prior, Louvain, 1904.

Cocchi, Guidus, *Commentarium in Codicem Juris Canonici,* 7 vols., 2 ed., Taurinorum Augustae, 1925.

Corradus, Pyrrhus, *Praxis Beneficiara,* Benetiis, 1735.

D'Angelo, S., *Parrocho E. Parrochia,* Giarre, Sicilia, 1921.

De Meester, A., *Juris Canonico et Juris Canonico-Civilis Compendium,* 3 vols., Bruges, 1923.

Denzinger, Henrico, *Enchiridion Symbolorum,* Edit. XII, Parata A Clemente Bannwart S. J., Friburgi, 1913.

Devoti, Joannis, *Institutionum Canonicarum Libri IV,* Leodii, 1860.

Devoti, Joan, *Institutiones Canonicae,* Romae, 1829.

De Luca, D. Joannis Baptistae Cardinalis, *De Beneficiis,* Coloniae Agrippinae, 1705.

Duchesne, L., *Christian Worship, Translated from third French edition by M. L. McClure,* London, 1903.

Ehses, Stephanus, *Concilli Tridentini Actorum Pars Sexta,* Eriburgi, 1923.

Engel, Ludovicus, *Collegium Universi Juris Canonici,* 9 ed., Venetiis, 1760.

Fanfani, Ludovicus I., *De Jure Parochorum,* Taurini, 1924.

Ferreres, Joannus, *Institutiones Canonicae,* 2 ed., 2 vols., Barcinone, 1920.

Funk, F. X., *A Manual of Church History,* 2 vols., London, 1910.

Gasquet, Cardinal, *Parish Life in Mediæval England,* London, 5th ed., 1922.

Garcia Nicolaus, *De Beneficiis Ecclesiasticis,* Venetiis, 1618.

Gamble, W. T. M., *The Monumenta Germaniae Historica: Its Inheritance in Source-Valuation and Criticism,* Washington, 1927.

Godfrey: *Right of Patronage,* Washington, 1924.

Golden: *Parochial Benefices in the New Code,* Washington, 1921.

Schulte, Fredericus, *Geschiecte der Quellen und Literatur des Kanons,* 3 vol., Stutgart, 1875, 1880.

Hedley, Bishop, O. S. B., *Lex Levitarum,* London, 1906.

Hefele, Chas. J., *A History of the Councils of the Church,* IV vols., Edinburgh (1883).

Imbart de la Tour, *Les Paroisses Rurales Du IV au XI Siecle,* Paris, 1900.

Kirch, C., *Enchiridion Fontium Historiae Ecclesiasticae Antiquae,* Friburgi, 1910.

Koudelka, Charles J., *Pastors, Their Rights and Duties, Washington,* 1921.

Lesetre, *La Paroisse,* 3rd ed., Paris, 1908.

Leurenius, Petrus, *Forum Beneficiale,* Venetiis, 1762.

Manning, Card. H. E., *The Eternal Priesthood,* New York, 1907.

Maroto, Philippus, *Institutiones Juris Canonici,* Romae, 1919.

Migne, *Patrologia Graeca,* 161 vols., Paris, 1857-1866.

Millet-Byrne, *Jesus Living in the Priest,* New York, 1901.

Monumenta Germaniae Historica, Berlin, 1826.

Mourret, F. S., *Historie de l'Eglise,* vol. 1.

Murray, Wm., *The Present Juridical Status of Parishes in the United States,* Washington, 1919.

Nardi, Luigi, *Dei Parrochi,* Pesaro, 1829.

Pallottini, Salavator, *Collectio Omnium Conclusionum et Resolutionum S. Concilii Tridentini,* 17 vols., Romae, 1889.

Petavius, Dionysius, *Dogmata Theologica,* Parisiis, 1867.

Pirhing, Enricus, *Jus Canonicum,* Dilingae, 1676.

Pistocchi, S. J., Marius, *De Re Beneficiali,* Taurini, 1928.

Prummer, Dominicus, *Manuale Juris Canonici,* ed. 3a, Friburgi, 1927.

Pugliese, J. M., *The Administrative Removal of Pastors,* Washington, 1927.

Raia, Salvatore, *De Parochis,* Romae, 1921.

Reiffenstuel, Anacletus, *Jus Canonicum Universum,* 7 vols., Venetiis, 1735.

Rossi, Joseph, *de Paroecia,* Romae, 1923.

Rouet De Journal, *Enchiridion Patristicum,* Friburgi, 1913.

St. Thomas Aquinas, *Summa Theologica Ex typ. Forzani* et S. Romae, 1894.

Sanguinetti, Sebastianus, *Juris Ecclesiastici Privati Institutiones,* Romae, 1884.

Santi, Franciscus, *Praelectiones Juris Canonici,* Ratisbonae, 1886.

Scherer, Rud, *Handbuch des Kirchenrechts Lips,* 1886-1898.

Schmalzgrueber, Franciscus, *Jus Ecclesiasticum Universum,* Romae, 1844.

Schulte, Fredericus, *Lehrbuch des Kath, Kirchenrechts,* Giessae, 1863.

Smith, *Dictionary of Christian Antiquities, Words, Parish and Patron,* Cutts, E. L., *Parish Priests and their people in the Middle Ages in* England, London, 1898.

Smith, S. B., *Elements of Ecclesiastical Law,* vol. 1, 5, ed., 1880; 2 vols., 1 ed., 1882; 3 vols., 3 ed., 1888, New York.

———, *The New Procedure in Criminal and Disciplinary Causes of Ecclesiastics,* 1888.

Soglia, Joannes, *Institutiones Juris Privati Ecclesiastici Libri III,* 7 ed., Parisiis.

Thomassinus, Ludovicus, *Vetus et Nova Ecclesiae Disciplinae,* Magontiaci, 1787.

Vacandard-Mangenot, *Dictionnaire de Theolique Catholique,* Paris.

Van Espen, Z. E., *Jus Ecclesiasticum Universum,* 2 ed., 2 vols., Cologne, 1715, *Opera Omnia,* 2 vols., Louvain, 1721.

Vecchiotti, Septimius M., *Institutiones Canonicae,* Taurini, 1868.
Vermeersch-Cresusen, *Epitome Juris Canonici,* Edit. 1927, III vols.
Villien, L'Abbe A., *Le Deplacement Administratif Des Cures,* Paris, 1913.
Waterworth, J., *The Canons and Decrees of the Sacred and Oecumenical Council of Trent,* London, 1848.
Wernz, F. X., *Jus Decretalium,* 3 ed., Prati, 1915.
Wernz-Vidal, *Jus Canonicum,* vols. II, V, VI, Romae, 1923.
Woywod, S., "*The New Canon Law,*" New York (J. Wagner), 1918.
———, *Patrologia Latina,* 221 vols., Paris, 1844-1855.

PERIODICALS

A Practical Commentary on the Code of Canon Law, 2 vol., New York, 1925.
American Ecclesiastical Review, Philadelphia, 1889.
Analecta Ecclesiastica, Romae, 1892-1911.
Apollinaris, Romae, 1928.
Canoniste Contemporaine, Le, Paris, 1878.
Revue des Questions Historiques, 1866 (1894-1896).
Revue Historique, Paris, 1876 (1894-1896).
Theologische Quartalschrift, Tuebingen, 1907, 1913, 1926.

UNIVERSITAS CATHOLICA AMERICAE

Washingtonii, D. C.

FACULTAS JURIS CANONICI

1929

No. 52

DEUS LUX MEA

THESES

QUAS

AD DOCTORATUS GRADUM

IN

UTROQUE JURE

APUD UNIVERSITATEM CATHOLICAM AMERICAE

CONSEQUENDUM
PUBLICE PROPUGNABIT

JOANNES JOSEPH COADY

SACERDOS ARCHIDIOECESIS BALTIMORENSIS

JURIS UTRIUSQUE LICENTIATUS

HORA XI A. M. DIE XXVIII MAII A. D. MCMXXIX

THESES

I.	De Dissertatione.	
II.	Canones 1–8	Normae Generales.
III.	Canones 8–24	De Legibus Ecclesiasticis.
IV.	Canones 25–30	De Consuetudine.
V.	Canones 31–35	De Temporis Supputatione.
VI.	Canones 36–62	De Rescriptis.
VII.	Canones 63–79	De Privilegiis.
VIII.	Canones 80–86	De Dispensationibus.
IX.	Canones 363–365	De Curia Dioecesana.
X.	Canones 366–371	De Vicario Generali.
XI.	Canones 372–384	De Cancellario Aliisque Notariis et Archivo Episcopali.
XII.	Canones 385–390	De Examinatoribus Synodalibus, et Parochis Consultoribus.
XIII.	Canones 423–428	De Consultoribus Dioecesanis.
XIV.	Canones 451–470	De Parochis.
XV.	Canones 471–478	De Vicariis Paroecialibus.
XVI.	Canones 479–486	De Ecclesiarum Rectoribus.
XVII.	Canones 492–498	De Erectione et Suppressione Religionis, Provinciae, Domus.
XVIII.	Canones 499–517	De Superioribus et de Capitulis.
XIX.	Canones 518–530	De Confessariis et Capellanis.
XX.	Canones 531–537	De Bonis Temporalibus Eorumque Administratione.
XXI.	Canones 539–541	De Postulatu.
XXII.	Canones 542–552	De Requisitis ut Quis in Novitiatum Admittatur.
XXIII.	Canones 553–571	De Novitiorum Institutione.
XXIV.	Canones 572–586	De Professione Religiosa.
XXV.	Canones 592–631	De Obligationibus et Privilegiis Religiosorum.
XXVI.	Canones 632–636	De Transitu ad Aliam Religionem.
XXVII.	Canones 637–645	De Egressu E Religione.
XXVIII.	Canones 647–648	De Dimissione Religiosorum Qui Vota Temporaria Nuncuparunt.
XXIX.	Canones 649–653	De Dimissione Religiosorum Qui Vota Perpetua Nuncuparunt in Religione Clericali non Exempta vel In Religione laicali.
XXX.	Canones 654–668	De Processu Judiciali in Dimissione Religiosorum Qui Vota Perpetua Sive Solemnia Sive Simplicia Nuncuparunt In Religione Clericali Exempta.
XXXI.	Canones 669–672	De Religiosis Dimissis Qui Vota Perpetua Nuncuparunt.

XXXII.	Canones 968–973	De Subjecto Sacrae Ordinationis.
XXXIII.	Canones 973–991	De Requisitis in Subjecto Sacrae Ordinationis.
XXXIV.	Canones 1094–1103	De Forma Celebrationis Matrimonii.
XXXV.	Canones 1104–1107	De Matrimonio Conscientiae.
XXXVI.	Canones 1108–1109	De Tempore et Loco Celebrationis Matrimonii.
XXXVII.	Canones 1110–1117	De Matrimonii Effectibus.
XXXVIII.	Canones 1118–1127	De Dissolutione Vinculi.
XXXIX.	Canones 1128–1132	De Separatione Tori Mensae et Habitationis.
XL.	Canones 1133–1137	De Convalidatione Simplici.
XLI.	Canones 1138–1141	De Sanatione in Radice.
XLII.	Canones 1142–1143	De Secundis Nuptiis.
XLIII.	Canones 1552–1555	Introductio in Librum Quartum.
XLIV.	Canones 1556–1568	De Foro Competenti.
XLV.	Canones 1569–1571	De Variis Tribunalium Gradibus et Speciebus.
XLVI.	Canones 1572–1579	De Judice.
XLVII.	Canones 1580–1584	De Auditoribus et Relationibus.
XLVIII.	Canones 1585–1590	De Notario, Promotore Justitiae, Vinculi Defensore.
XLIX.	Canones 1591–1593	De Cursoribus et Apparitoribus.
L.	Canones 1594–1596	De Tribunali Ordinario Secundae Instantiae.
LI.	Canones 1602–1605	De Signatura Apostolica.
LII.	Canones 1606–1607	De Tribunali Delegato.
LIII.	Canones 1608–1626	De Officio Judicum et Tribunalibus Ministrorum.
LIV.	Canones 1627–1633	De Ordine Cognitionum.
LV.	Canones 1634–1635	De Dilationum Terminis Fatalibus.
LVI.	Canones 1636–1639	De Loco et Tempore Judicii.
LVII.	Canones 1640–1645	De Personis ad Disceptationem Judicialem Admittendis et de Modo Confectionis et Conservationis Actorum.
LVIII.	Canones 1646–1654	De Actore et de Reo Convento.
LIX.	Canones 1655–1666	De Procurationibus ad Lites et Advocatis.
LX.	Canones 1667–1671	De Actionibus et Exceptionibus.
LXI.	Canones 1672–1675	De Rei Sequestratione et Inhibitione Exercitii Juris.
LXII.	Canones 1676–1683	De Actionibus ex Novi Operis Nuntiatiane et Damno Infecto.
LXIII.	Canones 1684–1689	De Actionibus Rescissoriis Et De Restitutione In Integrum.
LXIV.	Canones 1690–1692	De Mutuis Petitionibus Seu De Actionibus Reconventionalibus.
LXV.	Canones 1693–1700	De Actionibus Seu Remediis Possessoriis.

ROMAN LAW

LXVI. Roman Law—Sources and Value.
LXVII. Periods of Roman Law.
LXVIII. Jus Gentium—Jus Civile—Jus Honorarium, Jus Novum.
LXIX. Contents of Corpus Juris Civilis.
LXX. Personality and Slavery.
LXXI. Release from Slavery.
LXXII. Citizenship—Requirements and Rights.
LXXIII. Loss of Citizenship.
LXXIV. The Roman Family.
LXXV. Marriage.
LXXVI. Obligations in Genere.
LXXVII. Contracts in Genere, Evolution.
LXXVIII. Nature of Obligations.
LXXIX. Mutuum.
LXXX. Accommodatum.
LXXXI. Depositum.
LXXXII. Pignus.
LXXXIII. Verbal Contracts—Stipulation.
LXXXIV. De Dotis Dictione et Juramento Liberti.
LXXXV. Contracts in Writing.
LXXXVI. Universal Succession.
LXXXVII. Testate Succession.
LXXXVIII. Testamentifactio.
LXXXIX. Praetorian Wills.
XC. Wills under Justinian.
XCI. Praeteritio.
XCII. Querela Inofficiosi Testamenti.
XCIII. Legacies.
XCIV. Fideicommissa.
XCV. Influence of Christianity on Roman Law.
XCVI. Summum Jus, Summa Injuria.
XCVII. Jurisprudence.
XCVIII. Cognitio Extra Ordinem.
XCIX. Interpolations in The Corpus Civile.
C. Schools of Roman Law.

Vidit Facultas Juris Canonici:

PHILIPPUS BERNARDINI, S. T. D., J. U. D., *Decanus.*
LUDOVICUS H. MOTRY, S. T. D., J. C. D., a *Secretis.*
VALENTINUS T. SCHAAF, O. F. M., J. C. D.
FRANCISCUS J. LARDONE, S. T. D., J. U. D.

BIOGRAPHICAL NOTE

John Joseph Coady, son of Thomas Francis and Julia Cleary Coady, was born in the city of Baltimore, Maryland, July twenty-first, 1894. He received his early education under the direction of the Sisters of St. Joseph of Cluny, who at that time conducted but one school in that city. In September, 1907, he entered St. Charles College, Ellicott City, Maryland. This college was burned on March 16, 1911, and afterwards removed to Catonsville, Maryland. He was graduated from this institution in June, 1913. In the fall of the same year he entered St. Mary's Seminary, Baltimore, Maryland (chartered by the State as St. Mary's University). At this institution he received the degree of Bachelor of Arts in June, 1914; of Master of Arts in June, 1915, and of Bachelor of Sacred Theology in June, 1918. He was raised to the Holy Priesthood by the late Right Rev. O. B. Corrigan, former Auxiliary Bishop of Baltimore (from whom he had received all the other orders), on September 8, 1918. In the fall of that year he became professor of his Alma Mater, St. Charles College. During two years he taught English, Greek and Mathematics. He spent the summers of the years 1919 and 1920 as Curate to Monsignor Petri, Pastor of Our Lady Star of the Sea Church, Atlantic City, New Jersey. In the month of September, 1920, he went to Rome to continue higher studies in Sacred Theology, with residence at the Procure of St. Sulpice. He received from the Pontificial University, Collegio Angelico Internationale, the degrees of Bachelor of Sacred Theology, and Licentiate of Sacred Theology, June, 1921, and of Doctor of Sacred Theology, June, 1922. The subject of his doctorate dissertation was, *"De Causalitate Sacramentorum."* Upon his return to Baltimore in 1922, he was assigned as Curate to St. Matthew's Church, Washington, D. C., by the Most Rev. M. J. Curley, Archbishop of Baltimore. In that same year he enrolled as a student of the course in Canon Law under the direction of Msgr. Bernardini, and received the degree of Bachelor of Canon Law in June, 1923. In the fall of the year 1927 he took up again the courses in the study of Canon Law, which he had discontinued in 1923. He received from the Catholic University the degree of Bachelor in Both Laws, January, 1928; of Licentiate in Both Laws, June 1928. In partial fulfilment of the requirements for the degree of Doctor of Both Laws, he wrote and published this dissertation on The Appointment of Pastors.

www.ingramcontent.com/pod-product-compliance
Lightning Source LLC
LaVergne TN
LVHW050219080826
844660LV00012B/437

* 9 7 8 0 8 1 3 2 2 2 4 1 7 *